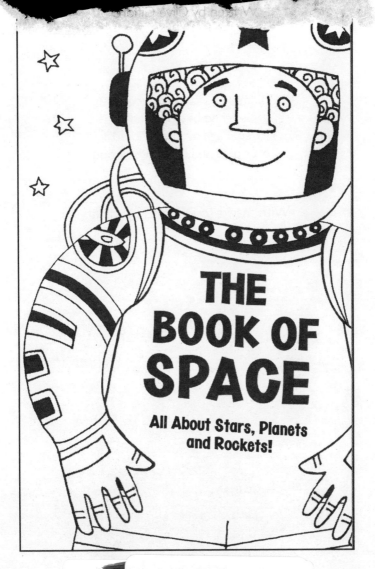

THE BOOK OF SPACE

All About Stars, Planets and Rockets!

Written by Clive Gifford

Illustrated by Andrew Pinder

Edited by Elizabeth Scoggins
Designed by Zoe Bradley
Cover image by Julian Mosedale
Cover designed by John Bigwood

With thanks to Dr Mike Goldsmith

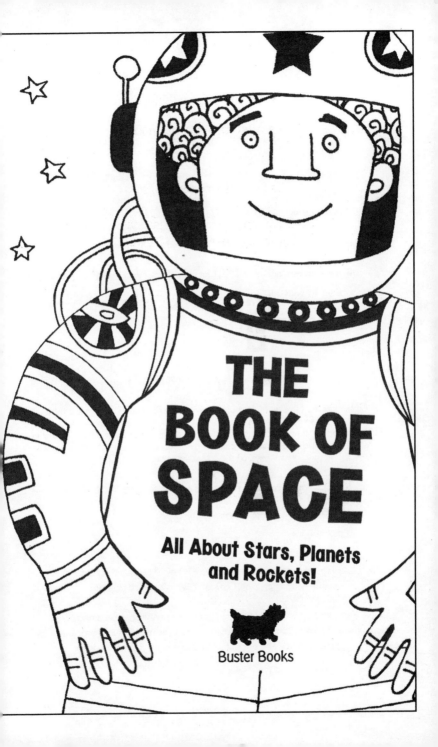

THE
BOOK OF
SPACE

All About Stars, Planets and Rockets!

Buster Books

This edition was first published in Great Britain in 2013 by Buster Books,
an imprint of Michael O'Mara Books Limited,
9 Lion Yard, Tremadoc Road, London SW4 7NQ

This is a paperback edition of a 2011 hardback book called *Out Of This World.*

 www.busterbooks.co.uk
 Buster Children's Books
@BusterBooks

520

Copyright © Buster Books 2011, 2013

A CIP catalogue record for this book is available from the British Library.

ISBN: 978-1-78055-139-5

1 3 5 7 9 10 8 6 4 2

Printed and bound in September 2013 by CPI Group (UK) Ltd,
108 Beddington Lane, Croydon, CR0 4YY, United Kingdom.

Papers used by Michael O'Mara Books are natural, recyclable products
made from wood grown in sustainable forests. The manufacturing processes
conform to the environmental regulations of the country of origin.

CONTENTS

If you've ever wondered what it would be like to walk on the surface of the Moon or wanted to pinpoint your place in the Universe – if you've ever dreamed of becoming an astronaut or hoped that one day you might meet an alien, look no further. This book will tell you everything you've ever wanted to know about space, from the edge of Earth's atmosphere to the edge of the Universe, if there is one.

See the sights of the Solar System, take a trip around the Milky Way, explore the Universe from beginning to end and find out what it's really like to live in space.

Get ready ... and ... liftoff!

THE EARTH, THE MOON AND IN BETWEEN

A Remarkable Rock

Earth is a rocky planet, the fifth largest in a group of eight planets that form part of the Solar System – all revolving around a star called the Sun. Nothing remarkable in that. After all, there are billions of other stars in the Universe, and plenty of far larger planets. Except Earth is the only known place in the Universe to support life – and that means you.

The world is remarkable, and for a long time people thought everything they could see in the sky – the Sun, Moon, stars and other planets – revolved around Earth. Understandable, really, but science has shown that things aren't so simple. Earth isn't the centre of the Universe, yet it is still incredible.

Planet Blueprint

You're about to read a lot more about Earth, so here are some of the most important bits labelled:

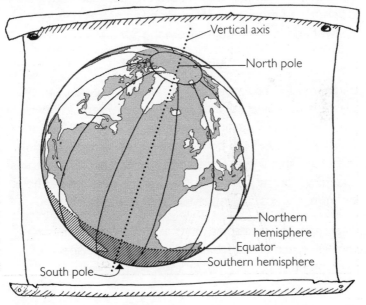

Quite A Waistline

If Earth was perfectly spherical, its diameter would be the same wherever you measured it. However, like many planets, it is slightly flattened at the poles and slightly wider at the equator – the imaginary line that runs round the middle of the planet. Earth is 12,756 kilometres in diameter at the equator, which makes it 42 kilometres wider than it is tall.

Round And Round

Earth travels round the Sun in an oval-shaped journey known as an orbit. Earth's average distance from the Sun is roughly 149.6 million kilometres, but this distance varies at different points in its orbit. The closest the planet gets to the Sun is 147.1 million kilometres, and the furthest it gets is 152.1 million kilometres – a difference of just 5 million kilometres.

This difference is not a huge variation compared to some planets. For example, Saturn's orbit means that it has a difference of more than 150 million kilometres between its nearest and farthest points from the Sun.

What A Spinner!

Earth may feel rock-solid and perfectly still to you, but the planet is actually constantly on the move. Every 23 hours, 56 minutes and 4.09 seconds, it completes a full 360 ° rotation on its vertical axis. To do this, the planet is rotating rapidly. In fact, it's spinning so fast that the surface at the equator is speeding along at approximately 1,670 kilometres per hour, or km/h – almost twice the speed of a jet airliner!

That's not all – as it spins on its axis, the Earth is hurtling through space on its orbit around the Sun at a speed of 30 kilometres per second, or km/s. Not impressed?

Well change that into kilometres per hour and you get 107,218 km/h. *Whoosh!*

At that rate, Earth completes an orbit once every 365¼ days – 365 days, 5 hours, 48 minutes and 46 seconds, to be precise. That's why, every four years, an extra day is added to the end of February to make a leap year of with 366 days instead of 365 to make up the difference.

Tilted

Earth doesn't move through space in a bolt upright position. It is tilted towards the Sun at a constant angle of 23.5 °. While the planet orbits the Sun, its tilt creates the seasons. As one hemisphere is tilted more towards the Sun for part of the journey, it enjoys its summer with warmer temperatures and more hours of daylight, while the other hemisphere is cast into winter. As the Earth continues its orbit, the seasons are reversed.

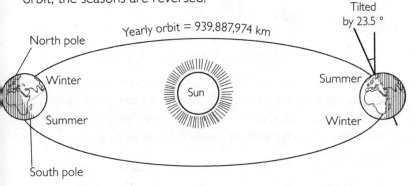

Tilted by 23.5 °

Yearly orbit = 939,887,974 km

North pole

Winter

Sun

Summer

Summer

Winter

South pole

Gravity Matters

Gravity is the force of attraction between objects. The smallest baked bean and the largest planet both exert gravitational force, but at vastly different amounts. This is because the more matter present in the objects, the more gravity. So an enormous object packed full of matter, such as the Sun, has enough gravity to attract massive yet distant planets hundreds of millions of kilometres away.

Cosmic Glue

The force of gravity is fundamental to how things hang together in the Universe. Gravity keeps moons orbiting planets and planets orbiting stars. It keeps galaxies together, including all their millions of stars, planets and other bits and bobs. And it stops you, and everything else on the Earth's surface, from flying off into space as the Earth spins. Pretty impressive.

How Much Does The Planet Weigh?

Earth tips the scales at 5,972,000 billion billion kilograms – roughly. However, the correct term for this is the Earth's 'mass', not its 'weight'. The reason for this is really important, so settle down for a short mass class – it'll be over very quickly, honest.

Mass Class

The mass of an object tells you how much matter it contains. An object can be quite small – a cube of gold, for example – but can have more mass than something much larger, such as a balloon. Wherever the object is found, on the Earth, the Moon or even floating in space, its mass never changes.

On the other hand, the weight of an object is the force caused by gravity pulling on the mass of an object. Gravity varies throughout the Universe. If you move an object to somewhere with different gravity, it will weigh a different amount. If you lob it out into outer space, far from any star or planet, it will have no weight at all. A person who weighs 60 kilograms on Earth would be 27 times heavier on the Sun. However, their mass would remain the same – although not if they had been burned to a crisp!

Earth	Moon	Venus	Mars	Jupiter	Sun	Space
60 kg	9.9 kg	54.42 kg	22.62 kg	141.84 kg	1624.32 kg	0 kg

Objects in orbit around the Earth or another planet have no weight either. On board spacecraft and space stations, objects can drift around if you are not careful. This situation is called weightlessness, but, to be perfectly accurate, there is a tiny amount of gravity present. This is known as microgravity.

Earth's Birth

Almost five billion years ago, an area within a large cloud of dust and gas – not far from where you are now – started shrinking and rising in temperature. As the cloud grew hotter and more dense in the middle, it started to rotate. It formed a giant spinning disc of colliding matter. Much of this matter was drawn into the centre of the disc and would one day become the Sun – the star at the centre of the Solar System.

Some Time Later ...

In a process lasting millions of years, the centre of the disc grew hotter and hotter, until it glowed with heat and light. It was now an object called a protostar, generating ferocious amounts of energy, which blew away most of the disc material. The leftovers continued to collide and join together into clumps. Eventually these clumps would become Mercury, Venus, Mars and Earth – the four rocky inner planets in the Solar System. At this time, there were as many as 30 planets around. Many of these crashed into one another and were either destroyed or joined together to form larger planets. In the end, only eight planets remained.

For a time, Earth's life was extremely violent. Vast volcanoes spewed lava, comets and meteorites bombarded the surface and the planet collided with other rocky objects. Over millions of years, things calmed down – the atmosphere (see page 16) took shape and large amounts of liquid water formed, providing the conditions for early life to flourish.

Water covers 70.8 % of the planet today, and helps support an incredible range of life. Scientists have already named more than 1.7 million different species of living thing and plenty more remain to be discovered.

Crusty Stuff

The Earth is made up of a number of layers:

Inner core
Iron, with a small amount of nickel and other elements – believed to be solid, incredibly hot and under enormous pressure – as much as four to five *million* times the pressure of the air pressing down on the Earth's surface.

Outer core
Liquid – mostly made up of iron, with a small amount of nickel and other elements.

Mantle
2,900 km thick, with an average temperature of over 1,300 °C – largely solid rock, but can bend and distort, like a piece of soft plastic.

Crust
8–40 km thick, floating above the mantle – made of rock.

I TOLD HIM NOT TO BURROW SO DEEP.

On The Move

Like the panels of a football, the Earth's crust is split into a number of giant pieces called plates. However, unlike a football's panels, these plates are edging away from, or over, their neighbours. They only move by centimetres each year, but with great force. It is their pulling away from each other or grinding together that creates the stresses and strains in rocks, which result in many of the world's most violent earthquakes.

15

What An Atmosphere!

Exosphere
Contains just a little
hydrogen and helium gas
– merges into space.

Thermosphere
Temperatures rise in the
thermosphere the further
away from Earth you go.

Mesosphere
Most meteoroids (see page
42) burn up in this layer.

Stratosphere
Rises to around 50 km
above the Earth's surface.

Troposphere
Extends from the ground
up to between eight and
16 km above the ground.
It is the most oxygen-rich
and is where the majority of
weather is generated.

An atmosphere is a layer of gases
surrounding a star, planet or moon.
Earth's atmosphere actually has
five different layers, giving the
planet ideal conditions to sustain
life. The atmosphere shields Earth's
surface from some of the Sun's
more harmful rays, yet lets enough
heat in to warm the planet. Clouds
of water vapour provide rain, and
the oxygen animals breathe in
helps them get energy from food.

For something that does so much,
Earth's atmosphere is surprisingly
simple. It consists of 78.1 %
nitrogen, around 20.9 % oxygen,
some water vapour, argon gas and
small amounts, or traces, of gases
including hydrogen, ozone,
methane, carbon dioxide, helium,
neon, krypton and xenon. Some of
these perform vital roles. For
example, ozone helps to absorb
and scatter a lot of the ultraviolet,
or UV, radiation energy that comes
from the Sun. Some UV rays still
reach the surface and can be
harmful to living things, which is
why you should wear sunscreen on
sunny days.

Are We In Space Yet?

It's tricky to work out where the exosphere ends and space begins. There is no clear dividing line and tiny traces of atmosphere extend up beyond some space satellites. According to the National Aeronautics and Space Administration, or NASA, in the USA, 122 kilometres is the level of altitude for re-entry. This is the height above Earth's surface where missions start to return to the atmosphere. However, many countries award 'wings' to any astronaut who travels over 100 kilometres above Earth.

Space Shuttle

What's Space Like?

With an average temperature of -270 °C, space is bitterly chilly – until you get near a star such as the Sun, where it is blisteringly hot. Space is also largely empty and deathly quiet, with only an occasional particle or gas atom for company.

Shhhh ...

Sound travels by making molecules of matter vibrate all the way into your ear. It can move through anything that contains lots of molecules – such as the air around you or a solid object, such as wood. Sound cannot move through space, though, because space contains next-to-no matter.

This is one reason that astronauts wear radios to speak to each other when outside a spacecraft. Unlike sound waves, radio waves can travel through space easily. They are then converted into sound signals inside an astronaut's helmet.

17

Next Door Neighbour

A natural satellite, or moon, is an object that orbits another, larger body, such as a planet, another moon or even an asteroid. Earth's only natural satellite is the Moon.

With a diameter across its equator of 3,476 kilometres, the Moon is 3.7 times smaller than Earth, but its mass is 81 times less. As a result, gravity on the surface of the Moon is about one sixth of what you are used to on Earth.

That's Whacky

Orbiting Earth at an average distance of 384,400 kilometres, the Moon is Earth's nearest neighbour in space and the only one that humans have set foot on. It has fascinated people from ancient times to the present day and astronomers are still wondering how it was formed.

The most common theory today is nicknamed, the Big Whack. It states that around 4.5 billion years ago, Earth was struck by a large object, possibly a giant asteroid or a protoplanet – a planet that is beginning to form. The impact destroyed the object, but sent much of its debris along with some of the Earth up into space. This cloud of debris gradually formed into the Moon.

No Cheese, Please!

You might have heard people joking that the Moon is made of cheese, but it's unlikely that anyone has ever really believed that. In fact, the Moon is made up of an inner core of metal, around 480 kilometres in diameter, surrounded by an outer core of rock heated so much that it is liquid. Surrounding that is a rocky mantle, which is topped by a solid rock crust.

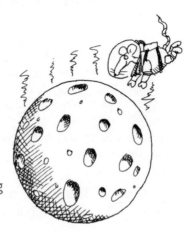

The surface of the Moon is covered in craters, which show where it was bombarded by comets and meteorites in the distant past. One of these, the Bailly crater, is roughly 300 kilometres wide and almost 4 kilometres deep. Another feature of the Moon's surface are large rocky plains called *maria* – Latin for seas. The largest is *Oceanus Procellarum*, meaning Ocean of Storms, an oval-shaped plain measuring around 2,500 kilometres by 1,500 kilometres.

Not Much Of An Atmosphere

For many years, it was thought that the Moon had no atmosphere at all, but in fact it does, although it's extremely thin. The Moon's atmosphere is made up mostly of neon – the gas used in some lighted signs, plus some helium, hydrogen and argon. Together, these four gases make up almost 98 % of the Moon's atmosphere, weighing just 25 tonnes in total. In contrast, Earth's atmosphere is thought to weigh around four million billion tonnes!

Long-Lasting Footprints

With so little atmosphere, the Moon has no weather and hardly any protection from the Sun. Temperatures on the Moon can swing wildly – far more than on Earth. According to NASA, the Moon's temperature can soar from as low as –233 °C to 123 °C – above the boiling point of water.

Without wind and water, the layer of lunar soil that covers large parts of the Moon's surface rarely moves. Chances are that any footprints left by the 12 astronauts who have set foot on the Moon during the Apollo Moon missions (see pages 100 to 101) are still there, along with quite a lot else.

Lost Property

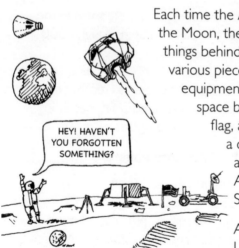

HEY! HAVEN'T YOU FORGOTTEN SOMETHING?

Each time the Apollo missions visited the Moon, the astronauts left a few things behind. These included various pieces of television equipment, a camera, some space boots, a hammer, a US flag, a golden olive branch, a commemorative plaque and golf balls hit by Apollo astronaut, Alan Shepard in 1971.

As well as all this, the Lunar Laser Ranging Experiment, installed in 1969, is still measuring the distance between the Earth and Moon. Using lasers, it has shown that the Moon is moving away from the Earth at a rate of 3.8 centimetres a year.

Does The Moon Have A Dark Side?

Only one side of the Moon is ever seen from Earth because it completes a full turn in the same time as it orbits the planet – 27.3 days. However, the other side of the Moon isn't dark. It gets the same amount of Sun as the side you can see.

Lunar Phases

A lunar phase is the amount of the Moon you can see from Earth depending on how much of it is lit up by the Sun. This amount changes each day. A complete cycle of the Moon's phases from new Moon to full Moon takes 29½ days.

Note: in the image below, each inner circle shows the angle of the lighted Moon to Earth, each outer circle shows how the Moon is seen on Earth.

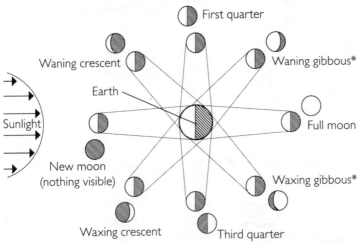

Just as Earth pulls on the Moon, the Moon exerts gravitational pull on the Earth. One of its main effects is to help cause bulges in the planet's water, pulling it up towards the Moon. As the planet turns on its axis each day, the bulge moves around the world, causing ocean levels to rise and fall, forming the tides.

* 'Gibbous' means that more than half the Moon is lit up.

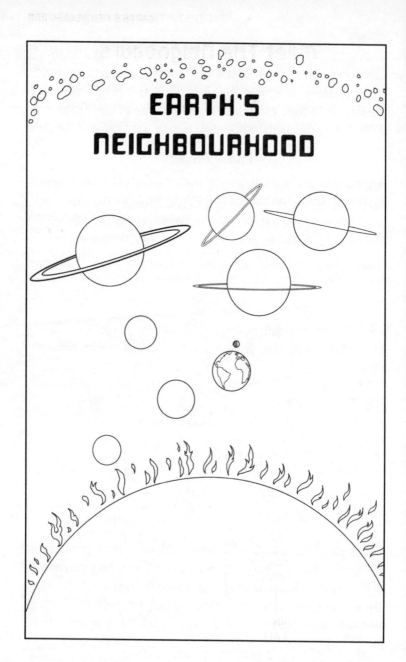

EARTH'S NEIGHBOURHOOD

Meet The Neighbours

As you already know, Earth is not alone. It is one of a group of eight planets in the Solar System, orbiting the Sun along with more than 150 moons, and various other bits and bobs.

Where Does It End?

Neptune is the farthest planet from the Sun, but the Solar System doesn't end there. The Kuiper Belt (pronounced *kye-purr*) is an area of space past Neptune, containing comets and dwarf planets, such as Pluto*, which stretches out to about 12 billion kilometres from the Sun. Beyond that is the Oort cloud, a giant area containing billions more comets.

How Far Is It?

For measuring distances on Earth, kilometres are great, but the Solar System is so large that the unit of measurement needs to be bigger – much bigger. The Astronomical Unit, or AU, is the average distance from the Earth to the Sun – 149,597,870.7 kilometres. This mega-measure is used a lot by astronomers to describe the distances in the Solar System.

Note: each number represents the planet's average distance from the Sun.

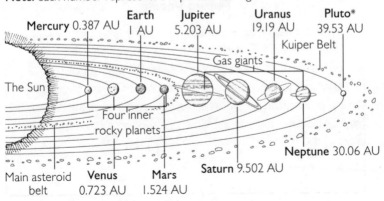

Mercury 0.387 AU

Earth 1 AU

Jupiter 5.203 AU

Uranus 19.19 AU

Pluto* 39.53 AU

Kuiper Belt

Gas giants

The Sun

Four inner rocky planets

Neptune 30.06 AU

Main asteroid belt

Venus 0.723 AU

Mars 1.524 AU

Saturn 9.502 AU

* Although Pluto was originally considered to be part of the Solar System, it was downgraded to a dwarf planet in 2006 (see pages 38 to 39 for more detail).

Sun Stuff

The Sun sits at the centre of the Solar System. This giant ball of gases burns away at unimaginably hot temperatures and has done so for almost 4.6 billion years. As it does so, it gives out vast amounts of energy, which provide warmth and light on Earth that enable the planet to support life.

Heavy Stuff

Although the Sun is a very ordinary star, with a diameter of approximately 1,392,000 kilometres, it is more than 109 times the diameter of Earth. Despite being made up of approximately 74 % hydrogen and 25 % helium – the remainder is a mix of other gases, the Sun has enormous mass and would be incredibly heavy if it wasn't weightless. It is estimated to have a mass of … wait for it … 2,000,000,000,000,000,000,000,000,000,000 kilograms, which is two *nonillion*, or 2,000 billion billion billion kilograms. That's heavy! You would need to load up 330,000 planet Earths on the other end of a seesaw in a giant galactic playground to balance that out.

Pulling Power

The more massive an object is, the more gravity it has, and the Sun is MASSIVE. It dwarfs everything else in the Solar System. In fact, the Sun contains over 98 % of all of the material in the Solar System – because it's so massive, its strong gravitational pull makes sure that large planets and any smaller bodies, such as asteroids (see page 39), keep orbiting around it.

A Giant Nuclear Powerplant

Unlike Earth, the Sun has no solid core or rocky surface, but scientists still divide it up into different layers or zones:

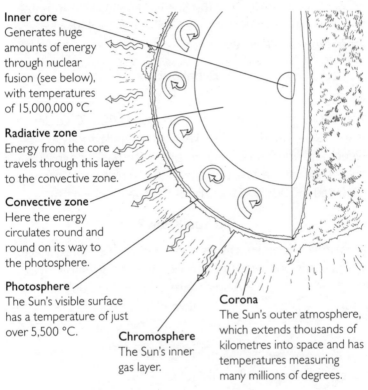

Inner core
Generates huge amounts of energy through nuclear fusion (see below), with temperatures of 15,000,000 °C.

Radiative zone
Energy from the core travels through this layer to the convective zone.

Convective zone
Here the energy circulates round and round on its way to the photosphere.

Photosphere
The Sun's visible surface has a temperature of just over 5,500 °C.

Chromosphere
The Sun's inner gas layer.

Corona
The Sun's outer atmosphere, which extends thousands of kilometres into space and has temperatures measuring many millions of degrees.

The Sun's core is very, very dense and although it only makes up 2 % of the Sun's entire volume, it contains about three-fifths of the Sun's mass (see page 13 for more on mass).

The temperature and pressure on the hydrogen atoms in the Sun's core literally rip them apart. The central part of hydrogen atoms, called the nucleus, then fuse, or join, with one another to form a helium atom. This releases vast quantities of energy in a process called nuclear fusion.

Will The Sun Ever Run Out?

To power its intense nuclear reactions, the Sun uses more than 600 million tonnes of hydrogen every second. This cannot go on forever and the Sun will eventually run out of fuel. You can relax though, a solar fuel shortage won't occur for another 5 billion years.

Breakout!

The Sun gets spots – sunspots. These are darker-looking areas of its photosphere, which are over 1,000 °C cooler than the surrounding areas. They can often last for days or weeks and are caused by disturbances to the Sun's magnetic field. They vary in size, but one of the largest ever observed occurred in 2003 and was about the size of 15 Earths.

Did You Know?

A solar flare is an enormous explosion on the Sun's surface, which sends out a blast of particles and energy into space. A solar flare observed in 2002 contained more energy than 5,000 million atomic bombs.

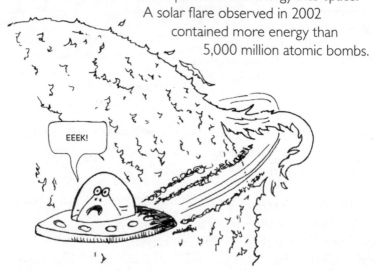

Mysterious Mercury

This little planet is named after the messenger of the Roman gods. The Romans believed that Mercury had feet with wings that made him super-speedy. Just like him, the planet Mercury is a seriously fast mover, the fastest planet in the Solar System, and the closest to the fierce glow of the Sun. It races around the Sun at an average speed of 47.87 km/s. At that rate, you could whizz across the Atlantic Ocean from London to New York in under two minutes!

Mercury is also the Solar System's smallest planet, and has just 5.5 % the mass of Earth. This means you would need 18 planets with the mass of Mercury to equal the mass of Earth.

Quite A Dent

Mercury has no atmosphere apart from a very faint trace of helium, so it doesn't get any wind or rain. This means that its surface, which is covered in craters and kilometre-high cliffs, has not been worn away. Its largest crater, the Caloris Basin, is thought to be where a huge object struck the planet over 4 billion years ago. It is roughly 1,550 kilometres wide.

Did You Know?

If you could stand on the surface of Mercury, the Sun would be three times larger in the sky than it is on Earth.

Mercury Stats

Distance from Sun: 46 to 69.8 million km
Diameter: 4,879 km
Mass: 330,000 billion billion kg
Rotation period (day): 58.6 Earth days
Orbit period (year.): 88 Earth days

Venus, Earth's Evil* Twin

The planet Venus has a relatively similar composition to Earth. Like this planet, it has a solid core made mostly of iron and nickel surrounded by a liquid outer core, then a rocky mantle and a crust on top. It is only slightly less dense than Earth and, at 12,104 kilometres in diameter round its equator, Venus is just 652 kilometres smaller than Earth. Above the surface lies a dense atmosphere. Gravity on the surface of Venus is about 90 % of what you experience on Earth. Doesn't sound too bad a place to be, so far …

Now The Bad News

Earth's atmosphere is mostly nitrogen and life-giving oxygen. Less than 1 % is carbon dioxide. In contrast, the atmosphere on Venus has next-to-no oxygen and is packed full of carbon dioxide – over 95 %, in fact, which acts as a thick blanket around the planet.

On Earth, small rises in the amount of carbon dioxide and other greenhouse gases in the atmosphere are known to contribute to global warming – the increase in world temperatures. On Venus, the atmosphere traps vast amounts of heat energy from the Sun. This means the temperature on the surface is the hottest of any planet, a scorching 465 °C – hot enough to melt lead.

* Well, not exactly evil, just not the sort of place you'd want to spend your summer holidays.

Under Pressure

If the heat on Venus wasn't bad enough, the atmosphere is worse. It presses down on the planet's surface with 90 times the amount of pressure of Earth's atmosphere.

An astronaut landing on Venus would be squashed flat in an instant while choking on carbon dioxide gas. That's if he or she had survived the descent through the upper atmosphere. Here, winds race at speeds of over 300 km/h and droplets of sulphuric acid pour down from heavy clouds.

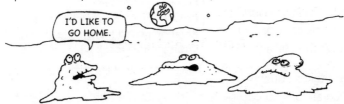

It all adds up to an unpleasant place even for a space probe (see pages 91 to 98 for more on these). These rarely survive more than a few hours in Venus's atmosphere. However one – Venera 13, sent by the Soviet Union in 1981 – lasted 127 minutes on the surface of the planet before conking out.

Star Bright

Venus gets closer to Earth than any other planet – around 42 million kilometres at its nearest point. This means it can often be seen from Earth and looks like a very bright star in the sky.

Venus Stats

Distance from Sun: 107.5 to 108.9 million km
Diameter: 12,104 km
Mass: 4,870 million million billion kg
Rotation period (day): 243 Earth days*
Orbit period (year.): 224.7 Earth days

* Unlike all the planets in the Solar System except Uranus, Venus rotates in the opposite direction on its axis to the direction it orbits the Sun.

Rocky, Red Mars

Mars is the last of the four rocky inner planets. For many centuries people hoped, or feared, that Mars was home to alien life. However, no Martians have ever been found by the more than 30 Mars probes sent from Earth. What scientists have found is that billions of years ago, water did flow across the surface of Mars. Any water that remains is locked in the planet's polar ice caps or just below the surface.

Mars Stats

Distance from Sun: 206.6 to 249.2 million km
Diameter: 6,792 km
Mass: 642 million million billion kg
Rotation period (day): 1.03 Earth days
Orbit period (year.): 687 Earth days

Mars takes roughly twice as long to complete an orbit of the Sun as Earth, but its day is almost the same as on this planet – lasting 24 hours, 37 minutes. However, with half the diameter of Earth and just over a third of the gravity, a human being landing on Mars would be 38 % of their usual weight.

Gravity on Mars may be weaker than on Earth, but it's still capable of keeping two small moons, called Phobos and Deimos, in its orbit. Many scientists think these were asteroids which got caught in the planet's gravitational grip.

Red Planet

Over 3,000 years ago, the Ancient Egyptians named Mars *Her Descher*, meaning 'the Red One'. The planet's colour comes from rocks rich in iron oxide, which is better known as rust. These rocks have been ground down over millions of years to form a fine, red soil that covers much of the planet's surface. Strong winds generate regular dust storms across Mars, which also give its atmosphere a red tinge.

Parts of Mars are covered in giant sweeping fields of sand dunes, but all that desert doesn't mean blistering-hot sun. The temperature on Mars ranges from a pleasant 20 °C on a summer day at the equator, to a decidedly nippy -87 °C on a winter's night at the poles.

Valley Deep, Mountain High

Mars has a couple of record-breaking features. First up: Valles Marineris – a gigantic system of canyons that have sliced into the Martian surface just south of its equator. The canyons are more than 4,000 kilometres long and are five times deeper than the Grand Canyon. If they were placed on Earth, they would stretch across the entire United States. That's big!

Olympus Mons is a 550-kilometre-wide volcano – the largest in the Solar System. It is estimated to stand over 25 kilometres high, around three times the height of Mount Everest, the greatest peak on Earth.

THAT'S A NICE LITTLE HILL!

Great Big Jupiter

There are no two ways about it, Jupiter is huge. It measures 142,984 kilometres in diameter at its equator and is so large that, if it were hollow, you could place 1,321 planet Earths inside and still have a bit of room left over.

If you added up the mass of all the other Solar System planets, Jupiter would still be 2.5 times greater.

Jupiter Stats

Distance from Sun: 740.5 to 816.6 million km
Diameter: 142,984 km
Mass: 1,899 million billion billion kg
Rotation period (day): 0.41 Earth days
Orbit period (year.): 4,331 Earth days

Cooking With Gas

Jupiter is one of the four planets in the Solar System known as gas giants. It is mostly made up of hydrogen and helium gas, but going down through its atmosphere, pressures and temperatures build, so that the hydrogen turns from a gas to a liquid. Scientists can't be certain, but at its very centre may lie a rocky core containing iron and silicon.

Even though it's a monster, Jupiter spins faster than any other planet. It takes only 9 hours, 56 minutes and 30 seconds to complete a rotation. This rapid spinning gives the planet a bulging waistline and flattened north and south poles – as though you were pressing a rubber ball between your palms.

The Great Red Spot

You might be fed-up if bad weather lasts a whole weekend, so imagine a storm that lasts continuously for 350 years. This is Jupiter's Great Red Spot, or GRS, which was first observed in the mid-17th century and is still raging to this day. Its winds swirl at speeds of well over 500 km/h. The GRS can be observed by amateur astronomers because it measures approximately 25,000 by 12,000 kilometres across. A second storm, half the size, but moving just as fast was discovered in 2000, and is known as Oval BA or Red Jr.

Many, Many Moons

A famous astronomer named Galileo Galilei (see page 66) discovered four moons orbiting Jupiter in 1610. Since that time, astronomers believe they have found another 59. Ganymede is the largest – and with a diameter of 5,262 kilometres it is larger than the planet Mercury.

Io is smaller, but fascinating, because it is seething with volcanoes, which send plumes of rock and dust as high as 300 kilometres above its surface.

Possibly the most exciting moon of all is Europa. Its icy surface covers liquid water and perhaps even some form of life below.

A Lighter Sort Of World

Next stop is the gas giant, Saturn, the second largest planet in the Solar System. Saturn's orbit is far longer than Earth's and takes an incredible 29½ years to complete. Yet at the same time, like Jupiter, Saturn spins fast, completing a 360 ° turn in 10 hours, 39 minutes. As a result, its shape is what scientists call an 'oblate spheroid' – flattened at its poles and bulging at the equator.

Saturn Stats

Distance from Sun: 1,352.6 to 1,514.5 million km
Diameter: 120,536 km
Mass: 568 million billion billion kg
Rotation period (day): 0.45 Earth days
Orbit period (year.): 10,747 Earth days

Floaty Light

There's no doubt that Saturn's a whopper, but despite its size it is actually the least dense planet in the Solar System. In fact, it's the only planet that would float in water, if you could find a pool big enough to try.

MUM, THERE'S A PLANET IN THE PADDLING POOL.

Lord Of The Rings

Saturn is famous for its rings, although Jupiter, Uranus and Neptune also have some, Saturn's are far and away the largest and brightest. The 275,000-kilometre-wide rings were first observed in the 17th century and are the only ones that can be seen with just a small telescope. Saturn has seven main rings, named A to G, and hundreds of thinner ringlets encircling the planet. They are made up of specks and chunks of water ice and some dust and rock. This matter reflects the light making the rings look like solid discs, but you could easily drive a bus through each ring's many gaps.

Mind The Gap

Speaking of gaps, a big fat one lies between Saturn's A and B rings, about 4,800 kilometres in width. It is known as the Cassini Division, after Giovanni Cassini, the man who discovered it all the way back in 1675.

A Cold, Cold Heart

The closest Saturn gets to the Sun on its travels is about 1,352.6 million kilometres, 9.5 times further away than Earth. This gives it a freezing surface temperature of around -140 °C. The planet is made up of around 95 % hydrogen gas, with helium making up almost all of the rest. Scientists think that below all of its layers of gas, there lies a rock and ice core around 12,000 kilometres in diameter.

Mighty Titan

Saturn has 53 known moons. Titan is its largest, and at 5,150 kilometres in diameter it's larger than Mercury. Titan excites astronomers because it's the only moon in the Solar System with a thick atmosphere, pressing down with about 160 % the force of Earth's – about the same pressure you'd feel at the bottom of a swimming pool. Titan's atmosphere contains argon, methane, carbon dioxide and hydrogen cyanide – that's right, the deadly poison, cyanide – but four fifths of its atmosphere is nitrogen. The only other body in the Solar System with a similar amount of nitrogen is Earth.

Tilting Uranus

Lying an average of 19.22 AU or 2,870,990,000 kilometres from the Sun, Uranus gets just 0.0025 % of the Sun's energy that Earth gets, making it oh-so-very cold.

Temperatures on its surface are estimated at below -200 °C, not that anyone is going to stand there with a thermometer in a hurry.

> **Uranus Stats**
>
> **Distance from Sun:** 2,741.3 to 3,003.6 million km
> **Diameter:** 51,118 km
> **Mass:** 86,800 million million billion kg
> **Rotation period (day):** 0.71 Earth days*
> **Orbit period (year.):** 30,589 Earth days

Not Your Average Seasons

Uranus has rings like Saturn and some 27 moons. It takes 84 years to complete an orbit around the Sun and, unlike other planets, is tilted on its side. This gives Uranus the strangest seasons in the Solar System. The area around the north pole, for example, faces the Sun for 42 years at a time, making it one long summer, while the south pole is plunged into darkness and bitter winter for the same length of time.

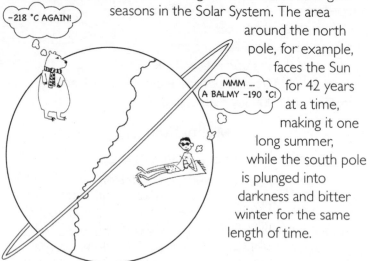

* Like Venus, Uranus rotates in the opposite direction on its axis to the direction it orbits the Sun.

No Birthdays On Neptune

If you think Uranus sounds grim, then check out a planet where you'd be over 164 in Earth years before you had your first birthday. That's how long it takes Neptune – the most distant of the eight planets to orbit the Sun. Its day, though, is shorter than Earth's. The planet spins on its axis once every 16.11 hours.

Neptune is the last of the four gas giants and its atmosphere is made up of hydrogen and helium. It also contains a little more methane than usual, which may be what helps give its clouds a blue colour when viewed by powerful telescopes.

When the Voyager 2 space probe flew by the planet in 1989, it discovered a storm the size of Earth, now known as the Great Dark Spot, moving at speeds of up to 2,400 km/h!

Neptune Stats

Distance from Sun: 4,444.5 to 4,545.7 million km
Diameter: 49,528 km
Mass: 86,800 million million billion kg
Rotation period (day): 0.67 Earth days
Orbit period (year.): 60,189 Earth days

Put The Heating On, Triton

Of Neptune's 13 known moons, Triton is its largest, coldest and most fascinating. It has the coldest surface temperature of any moon or planet in the Solar System, approximately -235 °C. Triton has an incredible surface with giant canyons, frozen lakes of ice and ammonia and ice volcanoes, which eject nitrogen and methane gas many kilometres upwards.

Poor Pluto

Poor old Pluto. After 76 years glorying in the title of the ninth and most distant planet in the Solar System, it was struck off the list and demoted to 'dwarf planet' status (see below). The former planet was discovered in 1930 by the American astronomer, Clyde Tombaugh, and is about two-thirds of the size of the Moon. On its 249-year-long solar orbit, Pluto never gets closer than 4.44 billion kilometres to the Sun. At its most distant, it lies around 7.395 billion kilometres away – over 49 times the distance between Earth and the Sun.

What's In A Name?

The planet was named in 1930 by an 11 year old British girl, Venetia Burney, who had been reading about the Roman god of the underworld, Pluto. Her grandfather got in touch with one of the astronomers trying to name the planet and passed on her suggestion, which she made over breakfast.

Just A Dwarf Planet

While it was still called a planet, Pluto was easily the smallest, with a diameter of approximately 2,300 kilometres – less than the width of Australia. Some astronomers doubted whether it should be the ninth planet at all and, when a new Solar System body called Eris was discovered in 2005, debate started raging. This was because Eris was the same size or a little larger than Pluto. Did that make it the tenth planet or were Pluto and Eris examples of a different type of object?

The International Astronomical Union, or IAU, is packed full of top astronomers who decide this sort of thing. In 2006, they chose to place Pluto, Eris and the biggest asteroid, Ceres, into a whole new group called dwarf planets. These are spherical bodies that orbit the Sun, but aren't big enough for their gravity to push aside the rock and other matter that might lie in their orbits.

Belt Up

Between Mars and Jupiter lies a doughnut-shaped belt containing millions of asteroids. These are usually irregularly shaped chunks of rock or rocks and metals. They can vary in size from a handful of metres to hundreds of kilometres across. Astronomers have named 15,000 and observed a further 200,000, all believed to be rubble left over from the Solar System's formation. Around nine out of every ten asteroids are found in the main belt, but groups are found elsewhere. For example, the Trojans are asteroids that orbit the Sun following Jupiter's path.

Dwarf-Planet Checklist
Basically spherical ✓
Orbits the Sun and not another planet ✓
Larger than a typical asteroid ✓
Big enough to clear the debris out of its path ✗

Not-So-Little

Ceres was the first asteroid to be discovered, in 1801, and was the largest until it was reclassified as a dwarf planet. The title now goes to Pallas which measures 570 by 525 by 482 kilometres. The surface of Pallas does not reflect light well, so the award of brightest asteroid in the sky goes elsewhere, to Vesta, which is the only asteroid you can see with the naked eye – without a telescope – from Earth.

Snowballs In Space!

Comets are large bodies regularly orbiting the Sun. They consist of frozen water and gases such as carbon monoxide, ammonia and methane, along with dust, metals and rock granules. It is because of this that they are often described as dirty snowballs.

Round And Round Again

Comets travel on large oval, or elliptical, orbits around the Sun. For long periods of time they are huge distances away from warmth, but as their orbits take them towards the inner planets, heat energy from the Sun causes some changes. They keep a solid nucleus at the centre, surrounded by a cloud of dust and gas called a coma, which is followed by a long, gassy and dusty tail.

What A Discovery

Comet Hyakutake was discovered in 1996 by a Japanese amateur astronomer named Yuji Hyakutake, using binoculars. Hyakutake caused great excitement as it passed within 0.1 AU of Earth two months later, allowing scientists to study the comet as it raced past at a speed of over 90,000 km/h. In 2000, Comet Hyakutake was found to have an incredibly long tail, some 570 million kilometres in length – about four times the distance between the Sun and Earth.

Where Are Comets From?

Astronomers believe that most comets originate in the outskirts of the Solar System. It is likely that they come from an area known as the scattered disc – some 30 to 100 AU from the Sun, or much further away in a region called the Oort Cloud, between 5,000 and 100,000 AU from Earth.

Like Clockwork

Hyakutake won't be back again in your lifetime. The comet was estimated to complete its orbit around the Sun once every 17,000 years. However, many comets have much shorter orbits and appear regularly in the night sky. The comet that orbits most often of all is Encke's comet, which completes its round trip once every 3.3 years. The most famous comet is Halley's comet, which was first spotted in 240 BC and returns every 75 or 76 years. It was sighted during the time of the Norman invasion of England over 940 years ago, and was even woven into the famous Bayeux Tapestry commemorating the Battle of Hastings in 1066.

BY THE SKIES! WHAT'S THAT?

Collision Course

A comet that met a tragic end was Shoemaker-Levy 9. In 1994, its fragments crashed into Jupiter's atmosphere at a speed of 216,000 km/h! The comet's path had been predicted in advance, which meant that for the first time, astronomers were able to witness the collision of two Solar System bodies. It lasted for five and a half days. One comet fragment struck Jupiter with 600 times more energy than all the weapons of the world detonating at the same time.

Meteoroid Or Meteorite?

Meteoroids are chunks of rock, dust and metal that enter the Earth's atmosphere. Most are fragments of asteroids but a few are small pieces of debris from Mars, the Moon or comets. So are meteorites, but there's a difference. The majority of meteoroids burn up in the atmosphere in seconds, melting and showing up as streaks of light in the night sky known as falling or shooting stars. Some larger meteoroids manage to survive as they travel through the atmosphere and fall to Earth. These are called meteorites and, so far, over 32,000 have been found all over the planet.

Ouch!

In 1954, an American woman named Ann Hodges became the first known person to be hit by a meteorite. It crashed through her roof and bruised her hip and hand. She was lucky – the meteorite that struck her weighed about 4 kilograms – about the same as a pet cat. The largest discovered meteorite was found in 1920 at Hoba West in Namibia and weighed over 54,000 kilograms.

Under Attack

The surprising news is that Earth is bombarded by stuff from space every single day. NASA estimates that between 1,000 and 10,000 tonnes of material reaches Earth every year, although most is microscopic granules of dust from the Solar System. Occasionally, larger objects such as comets and asteroids have struck Earth, leaving giant impact craters far bigger than the original object. For example, the 1.2-kilometre-wide Meteor Crater in Arizona is thought to have been caused by an impact object measuring just 30 metres across.

Did You Know?

Many scientists now believe that a massive asteroid impact in Yucatán, Mexico, was the reason that the dinosaurs became extinct. The impact, 65 million years ago, would have caused massive global flooding and volcanic activity. It would also have darkened the entire sky with dust, creating a worldwide winter.

Too Many Stars To Count

Most stars are huge spheres of hot gas held together by their own gravity. Other forces are also at work inside a star. The hot gas and energy generated at the core of the star tries to push outwards, while gravity tries to force the star to collapse in on itself. It's a little like trying to blow a balloon up while someone else squeezes the balloon tightly. The two sets of forces stay balanced throughout much of a star's life.

Enormous!

Stars are found along with gas and dust remnants of dead or failed stars, in sprawling areas of space known as galaxies.

Galaxies vary in size and shape, but all are enormous. The Solar System's star, the Sun, is far from being the only one in space. A small galaxy is thought of as one containing hundreds of millions of stars. Bigger galaxies contain billions. Astronomers think there may be as many as 100 billion galaxies in the Universe and possibly many more.

How Many?

If the truth be told, astronomers don't know how many stars there are in total. In the distant past, people used to think there were around a thousand stars in total. As telescopes and other scientific instruments have advanced, astronomers have been able to see much further into space and the estimated numbers of stars has gone up and up and up ...

In 2003, Australian astronomers estimated there to be a total of 70 sextillion stars in the known Universe. That's 70 followed by 21 zeros, so there are more stars in the Universe than grains of sand on all of Earth's beaches put together!

That number may not be the end of it. In 2010, astronomers using the Keck telescope in Hawaii announced that there may be three times more stars than previously thought.

Light Years Away

Astronomical Units, or AU, are fine when measuring distances inside the Solar System. However, the distances between stars and galaxies are so huge that a larger unit of measurement is necessary. Astronomers use 'light years' – a measure of how far light travels in a year – 9,460,528,404,847 kilometres – the same as 63,240 Astronomical Units. This means that light travels at almost 300,000 kilometres per second – enough to whizz round Earth's equator seven times!

The Sun's nearest neighbouring star is Proxima Centauri – 4.24 light years away, which is equal to 271,928 AUs. Travelling at 80 km/h, it would take around 56 million years to reach Proxima Centauri. Even travelling at 25,000 km/h – 30 times the speed of a jet airliner – would give you a journey of 181,000 years.

Time Travels

The extreme distances involved in space lead to some pretty mind-boggling ideas. One of the most important is that light takes the tiniest fraction of a second to travel across the room to reach your eye, but as distances increase, its journey takes longer. For example, light from the Sun takes eight minutes to reach Earth. This means that the Sun you see is actually the Sun eight minutes ago. See? Mind-boggling.

Light-Travel Time	Astronomical Units (AU)	Distance Travelled (km)
I light-second	0.002	299,792.5
I light-minute	0.1202	17.98 million
I light-day	173.14	25.9 billion
I light-year	63,240.2	9.46 trillion

Some of the stars and galaxies astronomers view are millions of light years away. This means that light from them takes a journey across space lasting millions of years to reach Earth. As a result, what you can see is how the star or galaxy looked when light first left it. It's as though your telescope has suddenly

SO IT WAS YOU THAT STOLE MY SWEETS WHEN WE WERE LITTLE!

DISTANCE FROM EARTH
25 Light Years

become a time machine, whisking you back in time millions of years. It's an important concept for astronomers who observe more distant stars and galaxies to view the Universe when it was much younger.

Life Of The Stars

Stars are born, live and die over lifespans measured not in centuries, but in millions or even billions of years. Earth's nearest star, the Sun, is approximately 4.6 billion years old. Astronomers have located stars in the Universe much older than this, including HE 1523-0901, which at 13.2 billion years of age, is the oldest known star in the Milky Way.

A Star Is Born

Most stars are born in enormous star nurseries called nebulae (pronounced *neb-you-lee*). A nebula is made up of giant clouds of gas – mostly hydrogen and helium – as well as large amounts of dust.

Astronomers think that this matter is mostly the remains of previous stars that have exploded or died. Some older stars, though, may have been formed from matter left over from the Big Bang (see pages 117 to 120).

The Orion Nebula is the nearest giant star nursery to Earth. It is huge and would take 50 light years to cross it from edge to edge. Astronomers have already found more than 150 baby stars in its clouds.

Protostars

Gravity causes matter in parts of a nebula cloud to pull together, shrinking in size, but increasing in density and heating up. The temperature and pressures build quickest at the centre, or core. This generates more gravity and pulls in more matter. As the spinning core collapses in on itself, it heats up more and more – it is now a baby star, a protostar.

Brown Dwarfs

Not all 'wannabe' stars make it. Some don't possess enough mass, a high enough temperature or enough pressure in their core to start off major nuclear fusion reactions (see page 25). These bodies continue to exist in space, but are very hard to see as their temperatures and their brightness is much less than stars that burn brightly – they are known as brown dwarfs.

The first brown dwarf to be discovered was Gliese 229B, in 1994. It is thought to be between 20 and 50 times the size of the planet Jupiter.

That's The Coolest

In 2011, what might be the coolest brown dwarf was observed, some 75 light years from Earth. CFBDSIR 1458+10B has a temperature of around 90 °C – about the same as a fresh cup of tea.

Star Quality

Once up and running, nuclear fusion at a star's core (see page 25) may last for billions of years. During most of this time – around 90 % of many stars' lives – it remains relatively stable and shines brightly. Space scientists say that the star is going through its main sequence, when it is burning hydrogen and creating helium relentlessly. The Sun, for example, has been in its main sequence for over four billion years, with plenty more years to come.

Bigger Stars, Shorter Life

You'd think that a star that is bigger, with more mass, would have more fuel to burn, and you'd be right. However, if you thought that that means it would burn for a much longer time, you'd be wrong. More massive stars tend to have far hotter cores, so the nuclear reactions occur at a much faster rate and they use up their fuel far more quickly. For example, a star with ten times the mass of the Sun is on its main sequence for only 20 million years.

Star Colours

Astronomers measure and group stars in a number of different ways – from their size and mass to their location, temperature and colour.

WOULD YOU SAY THIS STAR IS MORE YELLOWY-GREEN OR GREENY-BLUE, GEORGE?

A star's colour usually depends on its temperature. The coolest stars glow deep red, while the hottest are blue-white. Most stars can be placed in one of seven 'spectral types' according to their colour. These range from type O – the hottest (over 30,000 °C), down to type M – the coolest (3,200 to 2,100 °C). In order, the spectral types are O, B, A, F, G, K and M. The Sun is a type G star.

Giants And Dwarfs

Stars vary in size and in the amount of mass they contain. Many, many stars are smaller than the Sun, which is 1.4 million kilometres across, and some are a lot, lot bigger. Rigel, for example, is a spectral type B star around 400 light years away from Earth. It measures approximately 100 million kilometres across. One of the biggest known stars of all is an absolute monster. VY Canis Majoris, is a spectral type M star about 4,900 light years from Earth. It is around 1,800 to 2,100 times bigger than the Sun. If you plonked it into the Solar System, it's outer surface would stretch almost to Saturn.

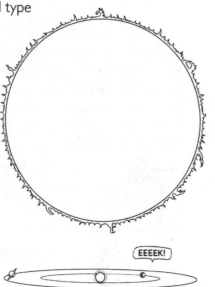

EEEEK!

Pipsqueak Stars

At the other end of the size scale are red dwarfs, which are tiny. They have between a tenth and half of the mass of the Sun and burn much less fiercely, which means that their fuel lasts longer. Proxima Centauri, Barnard's Star and many of the other closest stars to Earth are all red dwarfs.

Even Smaller

One of the smallest known stars is Ogle-TR-122b – not a very snappy name! It was found and measured using the Very Large Telescope, or VLT, in Chile, and has a radius of about 167,000 kilometres. That's only 20 % larger than Jupiter and not nearly as big as the Sun, which is 1,392,000 kilometres wide. However, because it is very dense and packed full of matter, its mass is around 50 times greater than the Sun.

Seeing Stars

There are up to 5,000 stars that can be viewed by the naked eye from different parts of Earth. In a clear sky, away from city lights, you might be able to see as many as 2,000 in one go. These stars can be seen partly because of how brightly they shine and partly due to their closeness to Earth.

Closest stars to Earth	Distance from Earth (light years)
Proxima Centauri	4.24
Barnard's Star	5.90
Wolf 359	7.80
Lalande 21185	8.30
Sirius	8.60

Star Measures

Astronomers measure how brightly a star shines in several ways. 'Apparent magnitude' is how bright a star looks to you on Earth. It's a slightly odd scale running from negative numbers (the brightest) to positive numbers (the least bright). Each whole number up or down means that a star is 2.5 times more or less bright. For example, Venus, the brightest planet in the sky, has an apparent magnitude of -4.4, while the brightest actual star outside of the Solar System, Sirius, measures -1.4. This makes Sirius 15.6

(2.5 × 2.5 × 2.5) times dimmer than Venus in the night sky. The Sun, of course, thrashes all other stars because of how close it is to Earth. It boasts an apparent magnitude of -26.7.

SO, SIRIUS IS SUPPOSED TO BE BRIGHT, EH? WELL I CAN'T SEE IT.

The second brightest star in the sky is Canopus, which has an apparent magnitude of around -0.6. The stars Arcturus and Vega have an apparent magnitude close to 0.0. This doesn't sound much to write home about, but that makes them the fourth and fifth brightest stars to be seen from Earth. The dimmest stars you can see with your naked eye have an apparent magnitude of +6.

Stars much farther away from Earth than Sirius and its neighbours aren't getting a fair deal with apparent magnitude, so astronomers use another measurement. This is called 'absolute magnitude' and is how bright a star appears to other parts of the Universe, from a set distance of 32.6 light years. On this scale, the Sun is +5 and not very bright, while the red dwarf, Proxima Centauri is really dim with an absolute magnitude of +15.45. Rigel is one of the brightest stars with an absolute magnitude of -6.69.

The Beginning Of The End

A star's fuel will run out eventually, even if it takes billions of years. As fuel at its core starts to dwindle, the size and mass of the star usually determines what its fate will be. For example, a red dwarf star with low mass may just slowly fade away, but if it is larger, a star tends to have a more complicated ending.

A Star's Fate

When an average-sized star like the Sun uses up much of the hydrogen fuel at its core, it starts to swell in size to become what is called a red giant. At this stage, the Sun would probably engulf Mercury and Venus and possibly Earth, too.

As it swells, the red giant starts to burn helium in nuclear reactions at its core. Its outer layers, still burning hydrogen, expand and glow more brightly. The star ejects much of its outer layers, which can form a nebula of gas clouds and dust matter. This is called a planetary nebula, although it has nothing whatsoever to do with planets. In time, this nebula drifts away, leaving a cooling star core called a white dwarf. These are small, but contain huge amounts of mass. A teaspoon of white dwarf would weigh over 13.6 tonnes! A white dwarf continues to shine for millions of years, slowly sending all its heat energy into space before fading away.

A Really Big Ending

When more massive stars, eight or more times greater in mass than the Sun, start to swell, they become supergiants. Betelgeuse (pronounced *beetle-juice*) is a red supergiant and an absolute whopper – between 300 and 700 times as big as the Sun and giving off thousands of times more energy.

As nuclear fusion runs out of fuel in a supergiant star's core, the core shrinks rapidly and temperatures soar as gravity forces the star to collapse. This usually ends in a giant explosion called a supernova, which blows most of the star's matter huge distances away and with great brightness. A supernova 6,500 light years away was observed by Chinese astronomers in 1054, and was bright enough to spot in the sky during the daytime for almost a month.

> INCREDIBLE! A STAR IN THE DAYTIME.

Did You Know?

A typical supernova explosion generates more energy than the Sun will produce throughout its entire 10 billion year life.

Neutron Stars

Some supernovas result in a dense core, which forms a 'neutron star' – one of the densest objects known in the Universe. A teaspoon full of material from a neutron star would have a mass of at least 100 million tonnes.

Some neutron stars spin rapidly and give off powerful radio waves which can be identified using radio telescopes. These stars are called pulsars. The fastest spinning pulsar so far has been given the strange name, PSR J1748-2446ad.
It whizzes round at a ridiculously rapid rate of 716 full spins every second, that's over 70,000 km/s – almost a quarter of the speed of light.

What's The Fuss About Black Holes?

First the not-so-exciting news: black holes are not portals to another Universe or gateways through which aliens can time travel. Well, scientists are pretty certain they're not, anyway. They are incredibly dense points in space where the gravity is so strong that all those laws of physics you have learned or will learn at school get thrown out of the window.

After some stars have been through a supernova (see page 55), their cores collapse in on themselves so much that they form a single, incredibly dense point in space called a singularity. The space immediately surrounding the singularity is called a black hole. Its force of gravity is so powerful that it pulls in everything that gets close enough. Once caught in its gravity, nothing can move fast enough to escape its grip, not even light. No one knows for certain what happens inside a black hole, but it's probably not good. Most scientists believe that gravity would crush anything that entered a black hole out of existence.

How Far Away Is Safe?

Black holes are extremely powerful close up but beyond a certain distance they no longer have the power to pull in and destroy. This boundary in space is called the Event Horizon and you would certainly want to be on its outside.

Hidden Holes

Light cannot escape from black holes, which makes them invisible – they were only discovered by studying the effect they have on things around them.

For example, a cloud of gas or a star passing close to a black hole can be torn apart by the black hole's gravity. As matter is pulled sharply towards the black hole, it speeds up and rubs against other matter, generating friction. This creates incredibly hot temperatures, as high as 1 billion °C and gives off lots of X-rays (see page 74), which can be detected as they travel through space.

THERE'S SOMETHING FUNNY GOING ON OVER HERE, GEORGE.

The first black hole to be discovered was Cygnus X-1 in 1971. It is thought to be about 30 to 60 kilometres in diameter, yet has the mass of as many as ten Suns.

Extremely Violent

M87 is a galaxy around 50 million light years from Earth. At its centre is a truly supermassive black hole, equal to 6.6 billion Suns – the most massive black hole yet discovered and measured. An enormous jet of gas and matter, over 5,000 light years long, is being ejected from this region of space at incredibly fast speeds – over 98 % the speed of light.

Home!

The Solar System's home galaxy is the Milky Way. It is a large galaxy, around 100,000 to 120,000 light years in diameter, containing at least 200 billion stars, and possibly, many, many more. The Milky Way features a central bulge, around 30,000 light years in diameter, surrounded by a disc around 1,000 light years in thickness.

Stars, gas and dust fan out from the centre of the galaxy in long spiralling arms. Branching off from one of these main arms is a smaller arm called the Orion Arm. This is where you would find the Solar System, some 27,000 light years away from the galaxy's centre.

Did You Know?

Just as the planets travel round the Sun, the Solar System orbits the centre of the Milky Way. It takes an estimated 225 million years for the Solar System to complete a full orbit. This means that if it completed an orbit today, it would have started it just as the dinosaurs were beginning their 160-million-year reign on Earth.

Are All Galaxies Spirals?

Many galaxies that scientists have observed so far – around two-thirds, in fact – are spiral-shaped, just like the Milky Way. These contain curving arms of stars and gases with a bulge in the centre. One of the largest spiral galaxies yet found – the Pinwheel Galaxy – is about twice as wide as the Milky Way.

Other galaxies form different shapes and these are used as a way of classifying, or grouping, galaxies into different types:

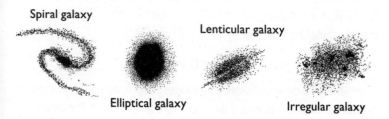

Spiral galaxy

Lenticular galaxy

Elliptical galaxy

Irregular galaxy

Elliptical galaxies are ball- or oval-shaped galaxies, which scientists believe are mostly collections of older stars. They are classed from E0 – an almost perfect circle – to E7 – a long thin oval. Lenticular galaxies have a bulge in the middle, like spiral galaxies, but no swirling arms. Irregular galaxies are those that have no obvious shape. Scientists believe some of them may have been pulled out of shape by passing close to or even through another galaxy.

A Sombrero, You Say?

One of the most photographed of spiral galaxies is the Sombrero Galaxy, which, with its bulging middle and large disc brim, looks a little bit like a Mexican hat. Lying 28 million light years from Earth, it is between 50,000 and 60,000 light years across and has a total mass equal to 800 billion Suns!

Cannibals, Collisions And Clusters

Galaxies collide occasionally throughout the Universe. Two similar sized galaxies may, over millions of years, merge with one another to form a new galaxy. Sometimes though, a large galaxy consumes smaller galaxies. This is known as cannibalism. The Milky Way's galactic neighbour, M31 Andromeda, is a notorious cannibal. Astronomers have observed it gobbling up dwarf galaxies because its powerful gravitational pull draws smaller galaxies in.

Star Burst

Cannibalism, or a collision of galaxies, can lead to significant amounts of the gas in a galaxy being compressed, heating up and igniting violently. This can result in a period of massive star birth. Starburst galaxies, such as the two colliding Antennae galaxies in the Corvus constellation, see huge numbers of new stars forming.

Collision Course

Most galaxies are moving further and further away from each other, but there's bad news for the Milky Way. It may be on a crash course with the infamous cannibal galaxy, M31 Andromeda, mentioned above. The gap between these two galaxies is closing as the galaxies move towards each other at a phenomenal speed of around 430,000 km/h. You can relax though – it will take two-to-three billion years for the two galaxies to collide, and then a further one billion years or so for them to merge into one giant elliptical galaxy.

Where Am I?

Galaxies themselves can be grouped together. The Milky Way and M31 Andromeda are part of a collection of galaxies known as the Local Cluster, or Local Group. This contains more than 30 galaxies, including the spiral-shaped, Triangulum galaxy and the Small and Large Magellenic Clouds, which, orbiting the Milky Way, are closer than most other members of the Local Group.

Astronomers have observed clusters in space with far more members though. The Coma Cluster, for instance, contains more than 1,000 galaxies. It lies around 300 million light years from the Solar System, but is so large that it takes light 10 to 20 million years to travel from one side to the other.

Everything in the Universe seems to be part of something bigger, and there's still one more stage to go. If clusters aren't big enough for you, how about superclusters? These are collections of groups and clusters of galaxies, again held together by the force of gravity. The Local Group is one of around 100 galaxy groups and clusters that are part of the Virgo Supercluster. This monstrous grouping is around 160 million light years from edge to edge!

So, your full address in the Universe is:

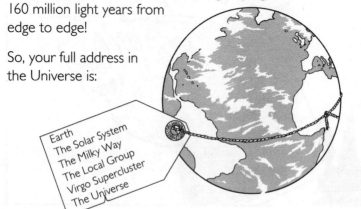

Earth
The Solar System
The Milky Way
The Local Group
Virgo Supercluster
The Universe

STARGAZING

Looking Up

Since the dawn of human history, people have looked up at the night sky with wonder and fascination. What were those twinkles of light too far away to ever reach and why did they change position throughout the year?

Many ancient civilizations all over the world watched objects in the night sky and plotted their movements. Some, such as the Babylonians, Mayans and Egyptians, used the Sun and Moon's movements to tell the time and construct calendars. Other cultures used the stars to help them navigate. The Polynesians were amongst the first people to use knowledge of where the stars were in the sky to navigate the Pacific Ocean on long sea voyages. Many ancient peoples, including the Babylonians, Egyptians and Chinese, thought that studying the night sky could help predict the future.

Risky Business

Astronomy in ancient times could be a dangerous business. Two Ancient Chinese astronomers, Hsi and Ho, failed to predict a solar eclipse in 2137 BC, over 4,000 years ago. Solar eclipses occur when the Moon passes in front of the Sun, casting a shadow on the surface of the planet. The Chinese believed eclipses were the work of a dragon devouring the Sun, so wanted warning. When the eclipse occurred without any warning, Hsi and Ho were executed for their failure.

Did You Know?

A 2,500 year old Ancient Chinese book, the *Book of Silk*, was discovered in a tomb in 1973. It contained drawings and details of the journeys of 29 comets, which the Ancient Chinese called broom stars.

Constellations

Different civilizations saw different patterns in the stars and grouped them together in different ways. However, in 1929, the International Astronomical Union forged worldwide agreement on there being 88 different star groups, or constellations. Many are named after characters in Greek or Roman mythology, such as Perseus and Andromeda. The stars in these constellations are rarely nearby in space, but they look as though they are when viewed from Earth.

Asterisms

Asterisms are small groups of stars that form a recognizable pattern in some constellations. These names aren't used by scientists, but amateur astronomers often use them to help them work out where certain stars are. For example:

The Big Dipper, also known as the Plough, is part of Ursa Major

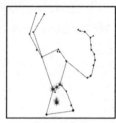

Orion's Belt is part of Orion

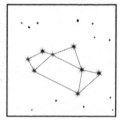

The Teapot is part of Sagittarius

The Fish Hook is part of Scorpio

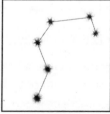

The Sickle is part of Leo

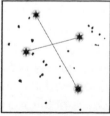

The False Cross is part of Vela

Stargazers

Early astronomers would produce catalogues of all the stars and planets they could see. In around 150 BC, a Greek scientist named Ptolemy published the *Almagest* – a book of 48 constellations, including 1,022 stars. Roughly 300 years before that, the Ancient Greek astronomer, Hipparchus, produced a star catalogue containing over 800 items. However, 200 years before him, Chinese astronomers had already recorded 1,464 stars. Star catalogues are still in use today, although these days they contain many, many more stars, much more accurately recorded.

The Man With No Nose

One man who spent much of his life staring at stars and constellations was Tycho Brahe. He was born in Denmark in 1546 and, as a young man, lost much of his nose in a duel with a fellow student. Brahe fashioned himself a new nose out of metal and went on to devote much of his life to building more accurate measuring devices with which to chart the night sky. His observatory on the island of Hven was rumoured to have cost the kingdom of Denmark 5 % of all of its money.

Brahe kept records of over 1,000 stars and planets, all observed by the naked eye, with a level of accuracy not beaten for more than 150 years. He also proved that comets were not parts of Earth's weather as most people believed at the time, but objects travelling through space.

Talking Telescopes

Early astronomers like Brahe would have bitten off your hand (or nose) for a telescope. Unfortunately, they weren't invented until about seven years after Brahe died, in 1601.

Making A Spectacle

Early telescopes, or 'spyglasses', were made by Dutch spectacle makers by placing two spectacle lenses at either end of a hollow tube. The lenses were able to gather in more light than the human eye and, when looked through, magnified the scene ahead, making objects seem closer. They became popular with sailors and spies as well as astronomers.

An Italian scientist, Galileo Galilei, built his own telescope in 1609, and used it to view sunspots. He also discovered that the Moon was covered in many more ridges and craters than can be seen with the naked eye. The following year, he found four moons orbiting around Jupiter. He also saw how the view of Venus changed each night and concluded that the planet must be spinning round the Sun.

Another famous scientist and astronomer of the time was Johannes Kepler. Kepler, who was Tycho Brahe's last assistant, went on to improve the design of the telescope, defend his mother in a witchcraft trial, and wrote the laws of planetary motion – the mathematical equations describing how planets move around the Sun.

Bending Light

Kepler and Galileo's spyglasses were 'refracting' telescopes.

Refracting Telescope

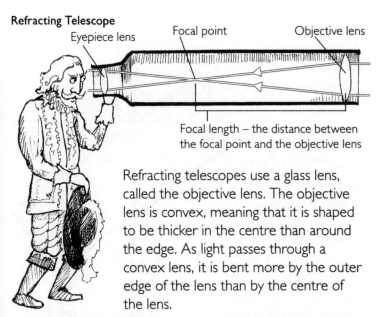

Eyepiece lens — Focal point — Objective lens

Focal length – the distance between the focal point and the objective lens

Refracting telescopes use a glass lens, called the objective lens. The objective lens is convex, meaning that it is shaped to be thicker in the centre than around the edge. As light passes through a convex lens, it is bent more by the outer edge of the lens than by the centre of the lens.

The lens then bends the light, so that it comes together, focusing inside the telescope at what is called the focal point. The light then passes through another lens in the telescope's eyepiece, spreading out across your eye, so that the focused image is magnified, in the same way a magnifying glass works.

Mirror, Mirror

Sixty years after the first telescope was made, the English physicist, Sir Isaac Newton built a whole new model. Instead of a glass lens, this used a mirror to capture light and then reflect it off another mirror towards a person's eye. Newton's first reflecting telescope had a focal length of just

15 centimetres, but magnified objects almost 40 times. For a refracting telescope to have the same power, it would need to be much bigger, with a focal length of between 90 and 180 centimetres.

Reflecting Telescope

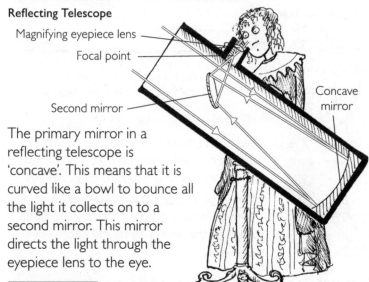

Magnifying eyepiece lens

Focal point

Second mirror

Concave mirror

The primary mirror in a reflecting telescope is 'concave'. This means that it is curved like a bowl to bounce all the light it collects on to a second mirror. This mirror directs the light through the eyepiece lens to the eye.

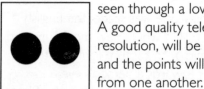

Low resolution

High resolution

The better the telescope, the better its 'resolution', which is its ability to see detail in an object. For example, two different points of light, such as two neighbouring stars, will blur together into a single point of light when seen through a low-resolution telescope. A good quality telescope, with high resolution, will be able to see more detail, and the points will be shown as separate from one another.

Bigger And Bigger

The bigger a telescope's lens or mirror, the more light it can gather in, allowing it to view fainter objects in the night sky. To create more powerful refracting telescopes, people built larger, heavier lenses and placed them further apart. In 1673, one keen amateur astronomer, Johannes Hevelius, finished an enormous 45-metre-long telescope. The King and Queen of Poland even visited. The problem was that it could hardly be used – the slightest breeze caused it to wobble!

Giant Reflecting Telescopes

Lenses get very heavy as they get bigger and can only be held in place at their delicate edges. As a result, the largest ever refractor, built in 1897 and still working at Yerkes Observatory in the United States has a 1-metre-wide lens that weighs a quarter of a tonne. In contrast, the mirror of a reflecting telescope doesn't need to let light through, so the rear of a large, heavy mirror can be supported. This means that reflecting telescopes grow to ENORMOUS sizes.

In South Africa, the hexagonal-shaped mirror of the Southern African Large Telescope, or SALT, is made up of a number of individual mirrors. In total, it measures 11 metres across at its widest point. If that's not big enough for you, the European Extremely Large Telescope, or EELT, is being planned to be working by 2018 and will feature a collection of mirrors measuring 42 metres in diameter. Giant!

Almost Perfect Precision

Today's biggest reflecting telescopes cost millions to design, build and operate. The attention to detail and accuracy is astonishing. For example, the gigantic 8.1-metre-wide mirror used for the Gemini telescope in Chile was polished smooth to an accuracy of 16 billionths of a metre. Its imperfections were so slight that if it was the size of Earth, its highest point would be like a hill that was less than 30 centimetres high.

Working Together

Also located in Chile, the Very Large Telescope, or VLT, is actually four separate telescopes, which can work on their own or as one. When they are used together, they are called an interferometer. The VLT's giant mirrors, each weighing 45 tonnes, were made by pouring a liquid material into moulds, then leaving them to cool gently for more than three

DO YOU GET THE FEELING WE'RE BEING WATCHED?

months. The VLT cost more than €330 million and its magnifying power is extraordinary. It could see the gap between a car's headlights if the car was on the Moon and it can spot a tiny firefly insect 10,000 kilometres away.

Why Chile?

After all that effort in construction, you want to make sure you put your giant, very expensive telescope where the bright lights of cities won't block out the stars. Nor do you want heavy clouds to get in the way at night. Chile, the Canary Islands in Spain and dry areas in the USA, such as Texas and Arizona are popular, 'clear sky' locations to site telescopes. Parts of Chile's Atacama Desert are so dry, scientists believe it hasn't rained for at least 20 million years. That's bone dry. As a result, it has some of the clearest, cloud-free skies in the world – perfect for stargazing.

Space Telescopes

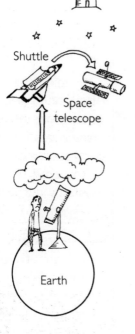

Shuttle

Space telescope

Earth

It's one thing to find an area with good, clear skies in which to place your giant telescope, but one step on from that is to get above Earth's atmosphere completely, and into space. As well as getting a better view of the stars, many space telescopes can also observe different types of waves, such as X-rays (see page 74), which the atmosphere absorbs, so they do not reach the ground.

Space telescopes take images using special cameras, then transmit the images and other measurements they take back to Earth using radio signals. Getting telescopes into space is expensive, so they must be well-designed, do a good job and be reliable – it's not that easy to make repairs!

Space Spectacles

The very first telescopes were made by spectacles makers. Almost four centuries later, the most famous space telescope of all, the Hubble Space Telescope, needed its own sight corrected.

Shortly after Hubble's launch in 1990, it was found that images from to Earth were slightly fuzzy. This was because the optical telescope's 2.4-metre mirror wasn't quite the right shape. In 1993, a Space Shuttle mission fitted it with COSTAR, a set of mirrors and a camera, the size of a baby grand piano, which acted as telescope spectacles.

Hubble Fact File

From a wobbly start, the Hubble telescope has gone on to become a really big deal in astronomy, showing people parts of the Universe they've simply never seen before.

The telescope has discovered the existence of supermassive black holes (see pages 56 to 57), helped scientists determine the age of the Universe and how it is expanding (see pages 117 to 119) and found many different galaxies and stars, including brown dwarfs. In 2006 alone, Hubble discovered 16 new exoplanets (see page 77) in other star systems and, in its first 20 years of operation, has taken a staggering 570,000 images of space.

Week-in, week-out, the Hubble has been sending back to Earth about 120 gigabytes of data every seven days – the same as filling a 1.1-kilometre-long shelf full of books. This data has proven very valuable to astronomers and scientists. Over 9,000 scientific reports and papers have been written based on the Hubble's work.

Cost at launch:
$1.5 billion

Length: 13.2 m

Weight: 11,110 kg

Power: 2,800 watts
– provided by solar energy

Orbit height above Earth:
569 km

Speed around Earth: 28,000 km/h

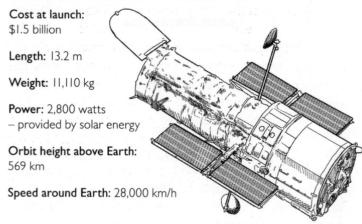

Seeing In Waves

Refracting and reflecting telescopes are optical telescopes – they collect visible light that can be seen with the human eye. Visible light is one of a number of different forms of energy that travel through space in waves. They are all part of the 'electromagnetic spectrum', which includes radio waves, X-rays and extremely powerful gamma rays (see below). Astronomers and scientists have found ingenious ways to capture and study these waves from space, using specially built instruments to find out more about the Universe.

Each wave type has its own length. Radio waves are the longest and can have wavelengths of many metres, while the waves of gamma rays are just one billionth of a metre long.

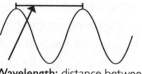

Wavelength: distance between equivalent points on a wave.

Extremely Energetic

Gamma rays can release more energy in ten seconds than the Sun will emit in its entire ten billion-year lifetime. They are lethal to living cells, but Earth's atmosphere absorbs almost all harmful gamma rays – good for humans, but not for gamma-ray astronomy. To study gamma rays, scientific instruments are sent into space or on high-altitude balloons, which travel above almost all Earth's atmosphere. Studying gamma rays help reveal some of the most violent parts of the Universe where massive high speed collisions between stars and galaxies occur as well as supernova, black holes and active galaxies.

Hot Spots

You probably know that X-rays can travel through flesh, so doctors can spot broken bones and other injuries, but they are also valuable in astronomy. They are emitted from objects in space, such as the remains of supernovas, that are hotter than 1,000,000 °C. In 1996, the ROSAT satellite discovered that even comets give off some X-rays. So far, over 780,000 sources of X-rays have been discovered.

Ultraviolet Rays

Ultraviolet, or UV, is a form of light with less energy than X-rays, but more than visible light. Many of the hottest stars in the Universe can be seen clearly in UV-light. UV-rays are emitted by the Sun and, like X-rays and gamma rays, are mostly absorbed by the Earth's atmosphere. UV telescopes sent into space have helped astronomers learn about young stars, as well as the areas of active galaxies filled with gases.

Infrared Rays

Your TV remote uses infrared rays, but in outer space infrared waves are given off everywhere. In many interesting areas of space, such as the centre of nebulae, large clouds of dust and gas block visible light. However, infrared rays aren't stopped by these clouds and can be seen by infrared telescopes either on Earth or in space.

One of the most successful space telescopes was the Infrared Astronomical Satellite, or IRAS. Launched in 1983, it discovered six new comets, many protostars, previously unseen dust clouds and a staggering 75,000 starburst galaxies. These are galaxies which give off large amounts of infrared energy because of the phenomenal numbers of new stars that are forming within them.

Radio Astronomy

Amongst the most important waves that astronomers can capture and analyse are radio waves. These are given off by many different bodies and phenomena in space – from sunspots to rapidly-spinning neutron stars. The waves penetrate Earth's atmosphere, meaning that large radio telescopes can be constructed on the planet's surface to gather in the waves for astronomers to analyse.

What's That Noise?

Radio astronomy began by accident when a telephone engineer, Karl Jansky, built a large and rather strange radio receiver mounted on a turntable, so that it could face in any direction. Jansky's 'Merry Go Round' was designed to investigate background noises heard in radio broadcasts. In 1932, he discovered that the background noises were in fact radio waves coming from space.

Few people took much notice, but six years later, an enterprising amateur astronomer, Grote Reber, built his very own large radio wave receiver – a 9.6-metre-wide dish – out of sheet metal in his own backyard. Reber discovered and mapped a number of radio wave sources in space, including strong signals from the centre of the Milky Way. Since that time, radio astronomy has

boomed in importance. It allows scientists to investigate parts of the Universe that cannot be seen – from star nurseries shrouded in gas to remnants of exploded stars. Radio waves also allow astronomers to trace where clouds of hydrogen gas are and how they are moving in different parts of the Universe.

Little Green Men

In 1967, a woman named Jocelyn Bell, who was a research assistant for radio astronomer, Antony Hewish, discovered a radio signal occurring every 1.337 seconds. She labelled it LGM-1 for Little Green Men! The signal turned out not to be from aliens, but from the first discovered pulsar – a rapidly spinning neutron star (see page 55).

Doing The Dishes

Large radio dishes gather in radio waves, which are then reflected on to a central point where an antenna changes them into electric signals. A radio receiver tries to amplify – meaning increase – the strength of these signals before they are recorded and analysed by computer. The world's largest single dish is in Arecibo, Puerto Rico, and measures 305 metres in diameter. An even larger dish, called FAST, which stands for 500-metre-aperture* spherical telescope, is under construction in China. When completed, it will have a radio-wave collecting area bigger than 30 football pitches.

One alternative to building bigger and bigger dishes is to build a number of dishes that all work together. This is called an array. The Very Large Array, or VLA, in the United States, for example, is made up of 27 radio telescopes arranged in a Y-shape. Each dish is 25 metres in diameter and weighs in at 209 tonnes.

* 'Aperture' is another way of saying width.

Searching For Aliens

Apart from the Little Green Men incident (see left), radio waves have genuinely been used to search for aliens – or to give them the scientific term: extra-terrestrial life.

In 1974, a message was beamed out in radio waves from the Arecibo dish in Puerto Rico. The message was aimed at a cluster of stars called M13, on the edge of the Milky Way about 21,000 light years away from Earth. If alien life-forms could recover the message and piece it together, it showed simple pictures of the telescope dish, the Solar System, a stick figure of a human and some of the key chemicals that act as building blocks to life on Earth.

Several long-distance space probes carry plaques or discs containing information about humans and Earth. Voyager I and II even carry a gold record, the size of an old-fashioned music LP (ask your parents) with sounds of nature and greetings from world leaders. Mind you, the chances of aliens having a record player to listen to it must be slim! Radio signals have also been beamed towards distant star systems and even at a large exoplanet – a planet that orbits a star in another solar system. Since the first exoplanet was discovered in 1995, there's been an exoplanet explosion. The Kepler space telescope, launched in 2009, has so far observed as many as 1,200 new possible exoplanets.

The Search Is On

The Search for Extra-Terrestrial Intelligence, or SETI, for short, is looking for aliens right now! Their tasks include analysing signals collected by radio telescopes to check for signs of alien existence or even any attempts at making contact with Earth. However, other groups also perform SETI activities – and you can join in, too.

SETI@home is an ingenious idea that launched in 1999. It allows people with a computer and an internet connection to participate in the search for extra-terrestrials. Huge amounts of data from the Arecibo dish needs to be sifted through and analysed by computers. The SETI@home program sends small blocks of this data to each PC, which analyses the data when the computer is standing idle. So, you can use your computer for all your normal tasks, then leave it to hunt for aliens while you have your tea.

Is There Anybody Out There?

People have long been fascinated with the idea of aliens, but scientists simply don't know if it could be possible for life to exist elsewhere in the Universe. Many feel that the search has only just started – it seems almost impossible that Earth is the only planet in the entire Universe to sustain life. However, scientists are yet to find even the merest hint of alien life and, even if life did exist elsewhere, it could be so far away that any form of contact would be impossible anyway. It's the ultimate needle-in-a-haystack search with the haystack being the size of the Universe!

If scientists were to find alien life, it would be in what is known as the 'Goldilocks zone'. Think of the fairy tale, where a fussy little girl tries different porridge, chairs and beds until she finds the one that is 'just right'. The principle for the Goldilocks zone is the same – just swap the porridge for a planet that's just the right distance from a hot star to be habitable. On a massive enough planet, this should allow liquid water and an atmosphere to exist, and let life, as we know it, to flourish. Exoplanets around the size of Earth in the Goldilocks zone are thought of as prime candidates for alien life.

Flying Saucer

Unidentified Flying Objects, or UFOs, have been spotted for thousands of years. Scientists believe that these can all be explained rationally. Many are believed to be weather phenomena, such as certain types of cloud or ball-lightning – others may be shooting stars, weather balloons or secret test flights of by military forces. Finally, some alien sightings and UFO photos are definitely hoaxes.

Pleased To Meet You

Exobiologists are people who study what life away from Earth might be like. Some argue that alien life may appear hugely different to what people think of as living things. After all, over millions of years, life on Earth has evolved in many specialised and ingenious ways. The planet you're standing on supports huge variety, from microscopic bacteria to 5.5-metre-tall giraffes and blue whales weighing more than 180,000 kilograms. Evolution on an exoplanet may lead to quite different results – especially if the gravity is higher or lower and if the atmosphere is different to Earth's.

DESTINATION: SPACE

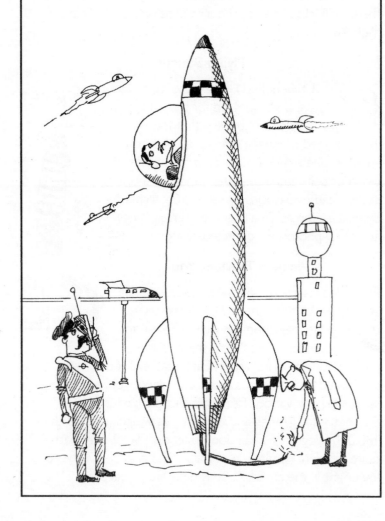

Escape Artists

Before you can explore space, you have to get to it. This involves being able to overcome Earth's gravity sufficiently, which isn't as simple as it sounds. The speed at which an object must fly to escape the pull of gravity is known as escape velocity. From Earth's surface, this is approximately 11.2 km/s – equal to an extremely rapid 40,320 km/h.

Aircraft can leave the ground because, as they slice through the air, their wings create faster-moving air above than below. The faster-moving air has lower pressure, and this generates the force of lift. An aircraft cannot fly into space though, as there is no air for the wings to keep generating lift. To get to space, a different solution is required … rocket science.

Fire Arrows

The first known rockets were fired at the Battle of Kai-Keng in 1232, almost 800 years ago. Chinese forces repelled Mongol invaders by launching 'fire arrows' – simple rockets using gunpowder as fuel. British forces in India were attacked by small rockets in 1792 and, by 1815, were using rockets themselves against Napoleon's armies at the Battle of Waterloo. Small rockets carrying a rope or line to shore could be fired over 300 metres to help a ship in distress. And by the early 20th century, scientists were turning their thoughts to how to use rockets to explore outer space.

2.5 Seconds

All early rockets used solid fuel, but in 1926, the American scientist, Robert H. Goddard, launched the world's first liquid-fuelled rocket. In a flight lasting two and a half seconds, it flew up 12 metres before crashing into a cabbage patch.

How Rockets Work

A rocket engine works on a principle first explained by the inventor of the reflecting telescope, Sir Isaac Newton. He wrote the Laws of Motion, and the third law states that:

For every action, there is an equal and opposite reaction.

What does this mean exactly? Well, when you push against something, it pushes back against you in the opposite direction with the same amount of force. For example:

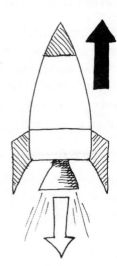

1. The thrust from a rocket engine pushes hard against the body of the launch vehicle.

2. If the rocket thrust is strong enough to overcome the force of gravity, the launch vehicle will lift off and rise upwards into the air.

Inside A Rocket Engine

Many rocket engines use liquid fuel, which they burn with oxygen-releasing substances, called oxidizers, to generate thrust. The fuel may be kerosene, gasoline or liquid hydrogen and is stored in a giant tank, or tanks, inside the rocket. The oxidiser, often liquid oxygen, is stored in one or more separate tanks. High speed pumps control the flow of fuel and the oxidizer into the combustion chamber where the substances are mixed together and ignited.

The fuel and oxygen burn quickly inside the combustion chamber, creating rapidly expanding gases. These swell out of the funnel-like nozzle at the base of the launch vehicle at eye-wateringly high speeds, often travelling at over 3,800 metres per second.

The enormous force of the gases thrusting downwards sends the launch vehicle upwards. As it travels further away from Earth the launch vehicle gets lighter and lighter in weight as it uses up its fuel and oxidizer at a rapid rate. The speed increases as a result.

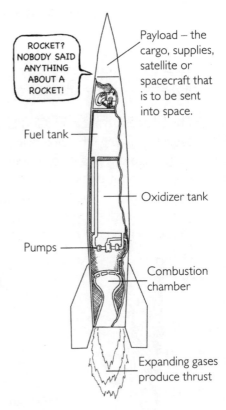

ROCKET? NOBODY SAID ANYTHING ABOUT A ROCKET!

Payload – the cargo, supplies, satellite or spacecraft that is to be sent into space.

Fuel tank

Oxidizer tank

Pumps

Combustion chamber

Expanding gases produce thrust

Need A Boost?

Many launch vehicles use solid-fuel booster rockets for extra power at the start of their journey. These are filled with pellets containing fuel and an oxidiser. Solid fuel rockets tend to be simpler to build and cheaper than liquid-fuelled rockets, but their thrust cannot be controlled. Once they start burning, they cannot be stopped. Solid rockets tend to use up their fuel within a couple of minutes after launch and are then dumped, or jettisoned, from the main rocket body.

Multi-Stage Rockets

Powerful launch vehicles able to carry a spacecraft high into space require huge amounts of fuel and liquid oxygen. This must also run through enormous engines to provide enough thrust. That's a lot of weight to carry.

The scientist, Robert H. Goddard was one of the first to suggest building what are called multi-stage rockets, with each stage carrying its own fuel and engines. As the first stage runs out of fuel and completes its thrust, it separates from the rest of the launch vehicle and falls away. The remaining rocket weighs less and requires less fuel and thrust to propel it on the rest of its journey.

The Biggest So Far

Nothing built and launched so far matches the might of the Saturn V multi-stage rockets for size, weight or power. These rockets were used to launch the Apollo missions to the Moon in the 1960s and 70s (see pages 100 to 101), and they were absolute monsters.

A fully-loaded Saturn V weighed 2,846,591 kilograms at launch. It stood 17.6 metres taller than the 93-metre-high Statue of Liberty and weighed a staggering 13 times as much.

The Saturn V was a three-stage rocket. The first stage was

powered by five hefty FI rocket engines, which together produced around the same amount of thrust as 32 Boeing 747 jumbo jets.

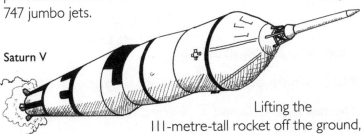

Saturn V

Lifting the III-metre-tall rocket off the ground, the first stage burned for 2 minutes and 47 seconds before falling away. Then the second stage, using five J2 rocket engines, took over for around six minutes. These powered the spacecraft up to an altitude – the height above Earth's surface – of 185 kilometres. Finally, the third stage, with its single J2 rocket engine, was used to propel the vehicle towards the Moon.

Gas Guzzler

Every second, each of the five FI engines on the first stage of the Saturn V rocket used 788 kilograms of kerosene fuel and 1,789 kilograms of oxygen.

Re-usable Launch Vehicles

Some parts of a launch vehicle, such as solid-fuel rocket boosters, are designed to land in the sea. They are then collected, refurbished and refilled, ready for use again. However, most parts are used once and once only. Only two reusable launch vehicles have ever been developed – the Soviet Union's Buran shuttle, which made just one flight, and NASA's Space Shuttle. Both look like aircraft, with stubby wings. They launch vertically, like a rocket, but return to Earth like an aircraft, gliding down to land on a runway.

Shuttle Mission Fact File

Shuttles: Columbia, Challenger, Discovery, Atlantis and Endeavour

Launches: 135 from 1981-2011

Orbit altitude: between 185 and 643 kilometres

Shuttles Lost: Columbia in 1986 and Challenger in 2003

Payloads: a total of over 1.4 million kilograms of satellites, scientific instruments, space station supplies and parts have been carried by shuttle missions.

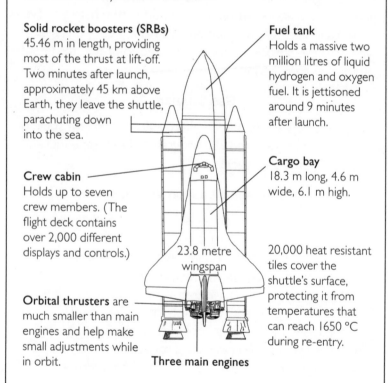

Solid rocket boosters (SRBs) 45.46 m in length, providing most of the thrust at lift-off. Two minutes after launch, approximately 45 km above Earth, they leave the shuttle, parachuting down into the sea.

Crew cabin Holds up to seven crew members. (The flight deck contains over 2,000 different displays and controls.)

Orbital thrusters are much smaller than main engines and help make small adjustments while in orbit.

Fuel tank Holds a massive two million litres of liquid hydrogen and oxygen fuel. It is jettisoned around 9 minutes after launch.

Cargo bay 18.3 m long, 4.6 m wide, 6.1 m high.

23.8 metre wingspan

20,000 heat resistant tiles cover the shuttle's surface, protecting it from temperatures that can reach 1650 °C during re-entry.

Three main engines

All Around The World

Artificial satellites are devices built by people to be sent by rocket or Space Shuttle into orbit around Earth. The very first, Sputnik 1, caused a sensation when it was launched in 1957 by the Soviet Union, which was a union of countries also known as the USSR. The USSR existed from 1922 to 1991, when it split into Russia, Ukraine, Georgia and a number of other nations.

Beep ... Beep

Sputnik 1 was a metal sphere about the size of a beach ball. It contained batteries, a thermometer and two radio transmitters that sent back a beeping sound, which could be heard by radio receivers all around the world.

SHE'S NOT VERY FRIENDLY, IS SHE, MARGERY?

Sputnik 1 completed an orbit around Earth every 96.2 minutes and sent signals back for almost 22 days before its batteries ran out.

Did You Know?

Over 2,000 satellites have been launched since Sputnik 1, performing a wide range of different jobs – from relaying television, telephone and internet data around the world, to monitoring the weather.

A Satellite Who's Who

Satellites orbit at different altitudes and can do a number of different jobs. Low Earth Orbit, or LEO, satellites travel from as little as 160 kilometres above Earth up to 2,000 kilometres. To avoid gravity pulling them back to Earth, they must race around the Earth at high speeds.

Medium Earth Orbit, or MEO, satellites are stationed on orbits more than 2,000 kilometres above Earth. They tend to cost more to build and launch than LEO satellites.

Are You Lost?

Orbiting at around 20,200 kilometres above Earth is a collection of 24 satellites working together, called a constellation. This satellite constellation provides the global positioning system, or GPS, navigations system used by sat-nav devices in vehicles. The time taken for signals to travel from a number of the satellites to a GPS device on Earth is used to calculate where you are on the planet and in which direction you are moving.

Keeping Pace

At an altitude of 35,785 kilometres above Earth's equator, a satellite takes the same time to orbit the planet as Earth takes to complete a full turn, so the satellite hovers in the same spot above the ground. This is known as a geostationary orbit, or GEO. These orbits are really useful for communications and TV satellites as signals can be beamed from one place on Earth to the satellite, which relays the signals to another point on the planet with almost no delay.

Spies In The Skies

Secret military satellites are thought to be able to spot an item as small as a grapefruit from space. They are used to spy on parts of the planet and to provide secure communications for troops. Some spy satellites also watch for missiles being fired or take high-resolution images of top-secret facilities.

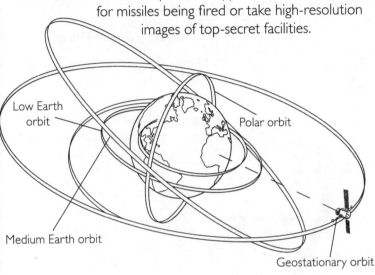

Low Earth orbit

Polar orbit

Medium Earth orbit

Geostationary orbit

Whatever The Weather

A number of satellites monitor the surface of Earth in different ways. Weather satellites monitor clouds, wind patterns and areas of cold and warm air that circulate the planet and generate weather. These are particularly brilliant at tracking giant storms that may turn into hurricanes.

Some satellites fly in 'polar orbit', studying landforms by moving above the planet's whole surface strip by strip as it turns. Several satellites take vast numbers of digital images, used in online global maps, while others measure the amount of moisture in forests, fields and other vegetation, or produce heat maps of the planet using infrared photography.

Goodnight, Satellite

When a satellite's life comes to an end, whether its systems fail or it stops getting power to its parts, mission controllers on Earth have a tricky decision to make. What do you do with a dead satellite?

A Very Grave Thing

Many satellites that have broken down, or have simply been replaced by newer, more advanced satellites, are put into what is known as a 'graveyard orbit'. Small rockets or thrusters on the satellite are fired to direct the satellite into a higher-altitude orbit, away from other satellites, to avoid collisions. One satellite currently cruising around Earth is Vanguard 1. Launched in 1958, it is still the oldest man-made object in space and has made more than 197,000 orbits of Earth. (See page 109 for more on 'space junk'.)

Other satellites are 'de-orbited' by directing them downwards, so that they break up as they re-enter the atmosphere. In very rare cases they are deliberately shot down by a missile. For example, in 2008, an American spy satellite, USA-193, had failed and was falling towards Earth. It was destroyed by a US missile some 247 kilometres above the planet's surface.

Far-Flung Things

Space probes are unmanned scientific machines. Unlike satellites they leave Earth's gravity and head out into space to explore a particular part of the Solar System.

What's On Board?

Probes vary in shape, size and complexity, but almost all have a number of features in common:

Radio antenna dish
Receives instructions from mission control on Earth and beams images and information back using radio waves. The further the probe is from Earth, the greater the delay between the signal being sent and received. Radio signals from the Cassini probe orbiting Saturn took around 80 minutes to reach Earth.

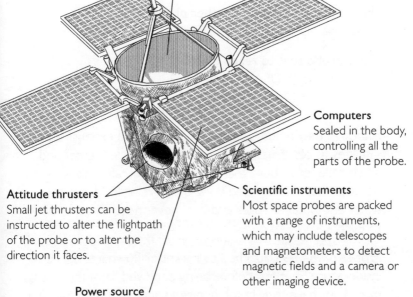

Computers
Sealed in the body, controlling all the parts of the probe.

Attitude thrusters
Small jet thrusters can be instructed to alter the flightpath of the probe or to alter the direction it faces.

Scientific instruments
Most space probes are packed with a range of instruments, which may include telescopes and magnetometers to detect magnetic fields and a camera or other imaging device.

Power source
Solar panels to generate electricity from sunlight.
Alternatively, some satellites use small nuclear power plants.

91

Space-Probe Firsts

First probe to land on a body other than Earth:
Luna 2, USSR, which crashed on to the Moon, 1959.

First probe to photograph another planet:
Mariner 4, USA, photographing Mars, 1965.

**First probe to land successfully on another planet
and send data back:**
Venera 7, USSR, on Venus, 1970.

First probe to reach an outer planet:
Pioneer 10, USA, which performed a fly-by of Jupiter, 1973.

First lander probe with a robot arm on another planet:
Viking 1, USA, on Mars, 1976.

First moving robot on another planet:
Sojourner, USA, on Mars, 1997.

First probe sent to reach Pluto:
New Horizons, USA, launched in 2006 to arrive in 2015.

Added Benefits

Although they tend to be more complex and expensive than satellites to construct, space probes are smaller, lighter and much cheaper to build than manned spacecraft. This is because they do not need crew quarters or food, oxygen, water and other supplies and they never need to come back to Earth.

Probes have been launched by rocket or flown into space inside Space Shuttles, before being deployed from their cargo bays. They have truly revolutionized scientists' understanding of the Solar System and many features of the Universe.

Probing Sorts

There are five main types of space probe. The kind used depends on what the target is – whether it is a planet or a moon that can be landed on, or a gas giant that must be flown past.

Fly-by probes take photos and measurements as they go past their main target. These spacecraft may only spend a short period close to their target planet or moon, so the amount of information they gather can be limited but still incredibly useful.

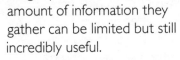

Mariner 10 managed three fly-bys past Mercury in 1974 and 1975, getting as close as 203 kilometres to the planet and photographing and mapping about 45 % of its surface. Some probes have performed fly-bys of different bodies in spaces. For example, Voyager 2 (see page 98) performed successful fly-bys of Jupiter, Saturn, Uranus and Neptune and is now heading out of the Solar System.

Orbiter probes are sent to a planet, moon or other body and then enter an orbit around their target. These probes spend far longer periods close to the body they are investigating, so can send back large amounts of data.

The Mars Reconnaissance Orbiter probe reached Mars in 2006, and is still orbiting. It has sent back more than 70,000 high-resolution pictures of the surface among its total of 17 terabytes of data. A single terabyte could hold 1,000 copies of the entire Encyclopedia Britannica – so that's a LOT of data!

The first orbiter around one of the gas giant planets was NASA's Galileo probe. Galileo finally got to work in 1995, after a six-year journey. It then spent eight years making 34 orbits, discovering many facts about Jupiter, its weather and its moons. These discoveries include the possibility of liquid oceans on Europa, and powerful volcanoes on another of its moons, Io.

Landers were sent to the Moon in the 1960s – either by the Soviet Union or the USA. Five American Surveyor probes made soft landings on the lunar surface.

HE'S ACCIDENT PRONE, SO WE BOUGHT THEM FOR HIM FROM NASA.

Many landers use small rockets that fire as the probe descends to cushion its landing. The Pathfinder probe to Mars, which carried the Sojourner rover (see below), used a parachute to slow the craft down. Then about 350 metres from the planet's surface a collection of giant airbags was inflated. These looked like a strange bunch of grapes, and surrounded the entire lander, protecting it as it set down. Once the lander and bags stopped bouncing on the surface, the airbags deflated and the probe could get to work.

Solar System planets and the Moon aren't the only targets of landers. In 2000, the Near Earth Asteroid Rendezvous, or NEAR, probe started its mission orbiting around the Eros asteroid, enabling scientists to study it in detail. At the end of its main mission, NEAR descended towards Eros and became the first probe to land successfully on an asteroid.

Rovers are able to move, or rove, around a planet or moon's surface on wheels or tracks to explore further.

The first of these were the Soviet Union's Lunokhod robot rovers, which landed on the Moon in 1970 and 1973, and were driven by remote control from Earth. The first rover on Mars, Sojourner, was a six-wheeled robot capable of slowly trundling across the surface, investigating rock and dust samples.

LEFT A BIT ...
RIGHT A BIT...

Lunokhod 1 was 2.3 metres long, ran on eight wheels and weighed a hefty 756 kilograms. The Sojourner Rover on Mars weighed just 11 kilograms.

Piggy-back probes are a two-in-one package, with a main fly-by or orbiting probe, which releases a smaller lander probe when it is close to its target.

95

For example, the Rosetta probe was launched in 2004 and is on a ten-year journey to reach Comet 67P/Churyumov-Gerasimenko. It will fly alongside the comet while dropping a smaller probe, Philae, to land on the comet's nucleus.

A Helping Hand

Many probes are not aimed in a straight line towards their target, but instead are sent on curving, looping paths close to a planet or the Sun, so that they can get a boost in speed from what is called gravity assist.

The first spacecraft to use gravity assist was NASA's Pioneer 10. It approached Jupiter at a speed of 9.8 kilometres per second, or km/s, and used gravity assist to move away from the planet at a speed of 22.4 km/s.

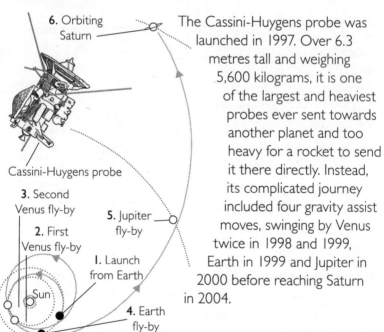

6. Orbiting Saturn

Cassini-Huygens probe

3. Second Venus fly-by

2. First Venus fly-by

5. Jupiter fly-by

1. Launch from Earth

Sun

4. Earth fly-by

The Cassini-Huygens probe was launched in 1997. Over 6.3 metres tall and weighing 5,600 kilograms, it is one of the largest and heaviest probes ever sent towards another planet and too heavy for a rocket to send it there directly. Instead, its complicated journey included four gravity assist moves, swinging by Venus twice in 1998 and 1999, Earth in 1999 and Jupiter in 2000 before reaching Saturn in 2004.

There And Back

Most space probes are launched from Earth on a one-way trip. With their mission complete, they continue travelling

through space or lie dormant – resting on the planet or moon surface they landed on. Some, such as the Galileo probe that orbited Jupiter, are instructed to crash into a planet or moon, sending back data to Earth right up to the moment they are destroyed.

A handful of space probes are programmed to return to Earth. For example, in 2004, a probe named Stardust encountered Comet Wild 2 389 million kilometres from Earth and collected samples of dust and gas from the comet's coma. Two years later, a capsule carrying the samples landed safely in the American state of Utah.

Mission Extensions

Some probes complete their main mission successfully and are given whole new tasks to perform, called mission extensions. The MER-B rover, Opportunity landed on Mars in January 2004, with a 90-day mission to study the planet's surface. It survived extreme temperatures and dust storms and was still working seven years later in Santa Maria crater, having travelled over 26,700 metres from its landing site.

Long-Distance Voyager

No probes have travelled further than Voyager 1 and 2. Launched in 1977, Voyager 1 is close to reaching 'interstellar' space – where the Solar System ends – at almost 18 billion kilometres away from the Sun. Voyager 2 is not far behind and on the way, it has discovered 11 new moons of Uranus. What's more, both probes are expected to have enough power to keep beaming back radio signals until around 2025.

Animal Astronauts

The first creatures launched into near space were fruit flies on board a V2 rocket launched in 1947. They reached an altitude of 103 kilometres. Since then, various countries have sent animals into space, mostly as part of experiments designed to test life-support systems for human astronauts.

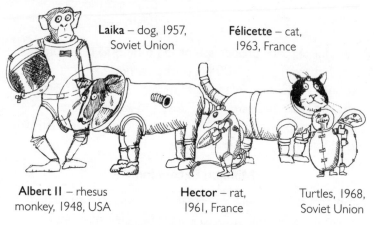

Laika – dog, 1957, Soviet Union

Félicette – cat, 1963, France

Albert II – rhesus monkey, 1948, USA

Hector – rat, 1961, France

Turtles, 1968, Soviet Union

Many Happy Returns

In 1961, a chimpanzee called Ham was sent into space. He had been trained to pull levers when lights flashed inside his capsule. Ham's capsule landed safely in the Atlantic Ocean and he received an apple and half an orange as a reward!

Space Race!

After the Second World War, the United States and Soviet Union were the two most powerful countries in the world. They vied with each other for top-dog status and this led to a race between the two nations to be the first to achieve many different milestones in space.

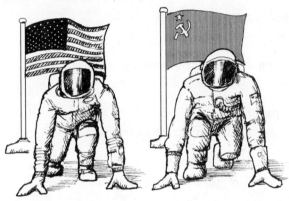

One of the most important aims was to be the first to get a person into space. A man named Yuri Gagarin was the one to achieve this in 1961. Gagarin was a test pilot from the Soviet Union who was chosen from 19 men who had all trained for the first space mission. He was strapped inside the cramped chamber of the tiny Vostok 1 spacecraft, less than 2.5 metres wide and launched into space on a historic single orbit of the planet. His whole journey from lift-off to landing by parachute took around 108 minutes and made him a national hero and global celebrity.*

Since then, more than 500 brave, smart and resourceful men and women have followed Gagarin into space.

* The battered Vostok space capsule that carried a dummy astronaut into space as a dress rehearsal three weeks before Yuri Gagarin's mission was sold at a 2011 auction for $2.9 million.

Astronaut Achievements

First woman in space:
Valentina Tereshkova, 1963, on board Vostok VI.

Most time in space for a man:
803 days, Sergei Krikalev – two stays on Mir, one on the ISS and two Space Shuttle missions.

First person on the moon:
Neil Armstrong, Apollo 11, 1969.

Most time in space for a woman:
376 days, Peggy Whitson – two stays on the ISS.

Most spaceflights:
7, Franklin R. Chang-Díaz and Jerry Ross, NASA astronauts.

Youngest person in space:
Gherman Titov, age 25, Vostok 2, 1961.

Oldest person in space:
John Glenn, age 77, Space Shuttle, 1998.

Competitive Spirit

Soviet successes stung the Americans into action. Their first astronaut, Alan Shepard, flew into space in the Mercury 3 spacecraft later in 1961. Ten two-man Gemini missions followed from 1964 to 1966. Gemini VII stayed in space for two weeks, an incredible record at the time.

The USSR responded by sending many of the first space probes to the Moon and Venus and building the Voskhod and Soyuz spacecraft. Two Soyuz vehicles performed the first docking between spacecraft in 1969. Soyuz spacecraft are still in use today as transport to the International Space Station.

To The Moon!

Of the 24 Americans who have orbited the Moon, half have stepped on its surface. Neil Armstrong from Apollo 11 was the first in 1969. The last was Eugene Cernan in Apollo 17 in 1972. Those 12 astronauts spent 80 hours in total on the lunar surface in missions watched by millions on television.

The Apollo missions were the most complex ever attempted at the time. Power came from the service module. The three crew members lived in the command module during the journey. Two astronauts went to the surface in the lunar module, while the other had to stay behind in the command module. To return, the top half of the lunar module blasted away from its base, skilfully docking with the command and service modules. The two astronauts transferred back to the command module and the lunar module was jettisoned into space. After journeying back to the edge of Earth's atmosphere, the service module was also jettisoned, leaving just the command module to descend through the atmosphere and splash down in the ocean.

Apollo Spacecraft

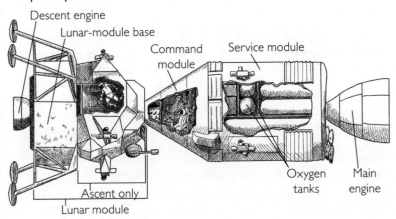

Descent engine
Lunar-module base
Command module
Service module
Oxygen tanks
Main engine
Ascent only
Lunar module

That's Space-Life

Living in space places many stresses on the human body. Luckily, the body is pretty good at coping and tends to re-adapt to life back on Earth not long after they return.

With no gravity forcing the spine down, astronauts grow by as much as 5 to 8 cm. This can cause back and nerve pain.

The body's fluids tend to rise upwards when they are not pushed down by gravity, often leading to a bulging neck and puffy face.

In the first minutes or hours of microgravity – where there is so little gravity that astronauts become weightless – many get space sickness, with headaches, tiredness and nausea.

Muscles weaken over time in space as they are not needed to support the body or to exert force as much as on Earth. Without exercise, they can grow flabby or shrink in size.

Your sense of smell is not strong in space, which is just as well, as only some spacecraft have showers.

The brain relies on signals from the inner ear and other parts of the body to know which way is up and which is down, and where all of the body's parts are. In microgravity, these senses can be a little scrambled, so astronauts can have difficulty with their balance.

According to a study of astronauts on the Mir space station, bones can lose as much as 20 % of their mass over long periods in microgravity.

By studying the effects on humans living in microgravity (see page 13), scientists have found ways to counter some of the effects. For example, to reduce muscle loss in space, modern astronauts exercise vigorously for a couple of hours daily.

Keeping Your Lunch Down

It's not easy to adapt to a lack of gravity, so astronauts are given the next best experience. Large planes fly up and down in huge curving flight-paths. Each time the plane dives down, people in the cabin briefly experience weightlessness. The astronauts use this time to learn how to move in space. Many first-time fliers report feeling disorientated and sick, giving the aircraft its nickname – the vomit comet.

If a vomit comet isn't available, you can also train under water. NASA's Neutral Buoyancy Laboratory has the world's largest indoor pool. It measures 61.6 metres by 31.1 metres, is 12.2 metres deep and holds 23.8 million litres of water. Full-sized models of a Shuttle cargo bay, or large parts of the International Space Station, can fit inside it. Astronauts can then practise manoeuvres in sessions often lasting 6 hours.

Suits You!

Astronauts don't need to wear full spacesuits and helmets all the time in space – cabins and modules are pressurized and full of air to breathe. Instead, they tend to wear things like overalls. These are often fitted with loops and clips, so that astronauts can fix themselves to part of the spacecraft and not float off. In addition, the clothing has lots of pockets for safe storage and Velcro pads so that useful items, such as notebooks can be kept firmly in place.

What's On The Menu?

Yuri Gagarin snacked on sausage and sweets as he whizzed around Earth, but most early space food was not quite so appetizing. Most meals were squeezed out of tubes, or eaten as bite-sized dry cubes. This way, there were no crumbs or droplets floating about to drift into astronauts' eyes or wreak havoc with air filters and instrument panels.

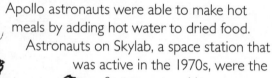

Apollo astronauts were able to make hot meals by adding hot water to dried food. Astronauts on Skylab, a space station that was active in the 1970s, were the first to eat real ice cream in space.

In 1988, the crew of the Mir space station were treated to a gourmet feast, including duck with artichokes and pigeon stew, by their guest, French astronaut, Jean-Loup Chrétien.

Just like on Earth, astronauts need a balanced diet containing the right vitamins and minerals. These days, each crew member's food is colour-coded and may include fresh food, such as fruit, but will also have many packaged foods. Meals are chosen well in advance of a mission and checked by dieticians. Some of the food is still dry though, so it weighs less when taken into space. On board the ISS, astronauts dine with magnetic metal trays to keep the cutlery in place, with Velcro strips to keep the food packs from floating off.

Don't Forget To Flush!

Microgravity certainly makes things interesting and what with things floating around going to the toilet is no exception! There were no toilets at all for the first astronauts who had to wear adult nappies inside their spacesuits.

These days, space toilets create a vacuum inside the toilet bowl to help your bottom form a good seal with the seat. Air from a powerful fan then moves the 'waste' neatly away.

WHO TURNED THE SUCTION UP?

In some spacecraft, astronauts sometimes still wear advanced nappies, or 'maximum absorbency garments', when in their seat ready for lift-off. After all, they may have to stay in position for hours before and during the launch period.

Washing in space is almost as tricky as going to the loo. In many spacecraft, astronauts wash with cloths and sponges and use special shampoo that doesn't need rinsing. Some spacecraft are fitted with ingenious space showers. To use one, you just seal yourself into the pod, so that no water can escape, take a shower, then use a vacuum-cleaner-style nozzle to suck up all the water droplets.

Cleaning your teeth is as important in space as it is on Earth, but a rinse and spit is not an option. Instead, NASA invented edible, foamless toothpaste that you swallow after cleaning!

Going Outside

If something goes wrong with a spacecraft or space station, it may be necessary to pop outside and fix it. That's right, outside in space. A spacewalk or to give it its technical name extra-vehicular activity, or EVA, can be performed to check on or repair damage to spacecraft, to help deploy satellites from a spacecraft's cargo bay or to monitor experiments.

To head outside, astronauts need to suit up and wear a complex, high-tech spacesuit. A spacesuit supplies oxygen, maintains pressure around the human body to keep everything in place and protects astronauts from particles whizzing around in space that might strike them. It must also provide protection from extreme temperatures, which can swing wildly from extreme heat to extreme cold, depending whether the spacewalk is in the Sun's glare or in darkness.

Air-Conditioned Underpants

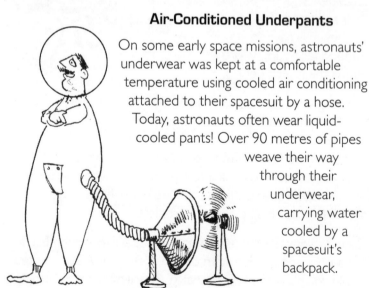

On some early space missions, astronauts' underwear was kept at a comfortable temperature using cooled air conditioning attached to their spacesuit by a hose. Today, astronauts often wear liquid-cooled pants! Over 90 metres of pipes weave their way through their underwear, carrying water cooled by a spacesuit's backpack.

EMU Suits

Astronauts wear an Extravehicular Mobility Unit, or EMU, to make spacewalks from the Shuttle and the International Space Station. It takes 45 minutes or more to put on and would weigh around 127 kilograms on Earth.

Spacesuits only ever come in white. This is because white reflects heat the most and also because it stands out against the blackness of space.

The primary life support subsystem, or PLSS, supplies oxygen and power, and cools the water running round the suit's layers, all in a handy back pack. Without it, an astronaut would fry and die.

The suit's helmet is mounted with a floodlight and spotlights to illuminate work areas outside. A video camera can film what the astronaut sees.

Spacewalking is thirsty work, but astronauts can sip from a small tube connected to a plastic pouch inside their suit, which contains 1.9 litres of water.

Heaters in the gloves warm the astronaut's hands.

The boots have soft soles to avoid damaging delicate parts of the spacecraft.

The bottom half of the suit, or lower torso assembly, includes the boots, trousers and knee and ankle joints.

Underneath the suit's outer layers, astronauts wear an electrical harness. This contains all the wires and connections to the radio and to instruments, which monitor the astronaut's heartbeat, temperature and other signs of their health.

Not An Everyday Stroll

Alexei Leonov performed the first ever spacewalk back in 1965. He spent 12 minutes outside his Voskhod 2 spacecraft attached to the craft by a 5.35-metre-long tether. He spent almost as long struggling to get back in through the airlock as his suit had over-inflated, but made it safely.

Nineteen years later, NASA astronaut, Bruce McCandless, became the first person to fly freely in space when he wore an MMU, which is short for Manned Maneuvering Unit. This backpack with arms contained fuel to power 24 tiny jet thrusters, which were operated with two joystick-like controllers placed close to the astronaut's hands.

In 2007, Susan J. Helms and James S. Voss performed the longest EVA in history when they were working on the International Space Station. They spent 8 hours and 56 minutes out in space – a real challenge, especially for Helms who was performing her first EVA. At the other end of the scale, no one is more experienced at spacewalks than Anatoly Solovyev who has performed 16 EVAs totalling a time outside in space of 82 hours and 22 minutes.

Whose Glove Is This?

In 1965, a spare thermal glove floated off into space from the second ever spacewalk. It's just one of over a million pieces of space junk orbiting Earth. Most are tiny, like paint flakes, but there is the occasional dead satellite or rocket fragment, too. Some of this is eventually drawn back to Earth and burns up on re-entering the atmosphere or lands on Earth.

Only one person is known to have been hit by a falling piece of space junk. Lottie Williams, a postal worker in Tulsa, USA, was struck a glancing blow on the shoulder by a piece of a falling Delta rocket in 1997. She was unhurt.

Scientists are more concerned about space junk colliding with satellites and other spacecraft. Even the tiniest fragment can cause damage because of the speed it is travelling at. In Low Earth Orbit, space junk can be whizzing by at a speed of 7.5 km/s – ten times faster than a bullet fired from a gun.

Oops!

During a 2008 spacewalk to make repairs to the ISS, a grease gun in Heide Stefanyshyn-Piper's tool bag leaked. While trying to clean up the mess, the tool bag, worth around $100,000, floated away and was lost. It was tracked through space and was spotted re-entering the Earth's atmosphere the following year.

Home From Home

The very first space station was Salyut 1, launched by the Soviet Union in 1971. Salyut has since been followed by three more space stations, which have been manned successfully. These orbiting space laboratories provide perfect conditions to perform all sorts of cutting-edge scientific research – from observing Earth in detail to building perfect crystals in microgravity. Experiments in space have led to new drugs to combat diseases and far more powerful computer processors.

The longest ever Space Shuttle mission, STS80, lasted 17½ days. Most manned missions on board the Space Shuttle and other spacecraft such as Soyuz last less than this, but by building space stations that orbit Earth people can live and work in space for longer periods at a time. Docking ports fitted to space stations allow spacecraft to ferry supplies, equipment and astronauts to and from the space station.

In 1994, Valeri Poliakov blasted off on his way to the Mir space station. He spent a record 437.7 days there – the longest continuous spell in space – before returning safely.

All Together Now

The first major collaboration between countries in space was the International Space Station, or ISS. It was built by the USA, Russia, Canada, Japan, Brazil and the European Space Agency. Its many modules fitted to the truss (see diagram) provide more living space than a typical five bedroomed house for the crew of up to seven astronauts. From 2000, when the ISS was first habitable, to 2010, 196 astronauts from eight different nations have visited the space station.

One Big Building Site

Space stations can be sent into space in one piece, but the ISS was different. In 1998, work began on the biggest ever building site in space. Over the following 12 years, more than 100 rocket and shuttle launches from Earth helped to assemble the International Space Station module-by-module, piece-by-piece.

The whole ISS covers an area roughly the size of a football pitch. It has travelled over 2.7 billion kilometres as it has made more than 68,500 orbits around Earth.

The International Space Station (ISS)

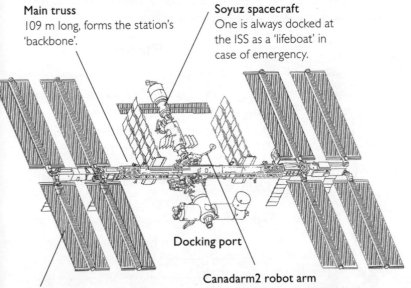

Main truss
109 m long, forms the station's 'backbone'.

Soyuz spacecraft
One is always docked at the ISS as a 'lifeboat' in case of emergency.

Docking port

Solar arrays
73 m long, provide electric power for the ISS from solar energy.

Canadarm2 robot arm
17.6 m long, helps handle objects with a mass of up to 116,000 kg. Sometimes, astronauts ride on the arm around the outside of the space station.

What Do You Do On The ISS?

Each day on the ISS is busy, busy, busy. Simple tasks such as washing, shaving and going to the toilet take far longer than on Earth. Everyone on the ISS must also exercise for around two hours each day to look after their muscles, using the space station's exercise bike and two treadmills. In between, there are many tasks to perform. This can be anything from maintaining the different parts of the space station to working on the many – often more than 50 – major science experiments and scientific instruments carried on board.

In their spare time, many space station dwellers read, watch DVDs, write emails home to family and friends or just gaze at the amazing, ever-changing view of home.

Phew-ee!

At least there's no washing to do on the ISS. Trousers are changed weekly and underwear every two days with the dirty laundry sealed in airtight plastic bags.

LAUNDRY

Checkmate, Chamitoff

In 2008, astronaut Greg Chamitoff played a game of chess on board the ISS against six mission control stations back on Earth. His chess set was fitted with Velcro, so the pieces didn't float off. Chamitoff won, but a few weeks later he suffered his first defeat in space when he lost a further chess game, this time against a group of American schoolchildren!

Space Vacations

In 2001, Dennis Tito, a billionaire businessman, checked in to the world's most expensive hotel – the Mir space station. Tito paid almost $3 million a night for his seven-night stay on Mir – the cost of going down in history as the first ever space tourist. Just a handful of other individuals have enjoyed 'holidays' in space since.

Plans for new spacecraft to carry more tourists into space are well underway. In 2004, SpaceShipOne became the first space vehicle built by a private company to climb over 100 kilometres above Earth's surface. SpaceShipTwo followed, completing its first test flight in April 2013. It is planned to be the first ever spaceliner carrying passengers. Each will pay around $200,000, for a short hop up into space.

Where Next?

The furthest people have travelled in space is to the Moon and back. It's not impossible that missions will ever travel further, but there are massive problems to solve. Travelling to Mars for example would take at least eight months each way, plus time to explore the planet. All the food, water and other supplies needed to live for three or four years would need to go, too – an enormous amount to ferry into space.

HOW IT ALL BEGAN ...
AND HOW IT MIGHT END

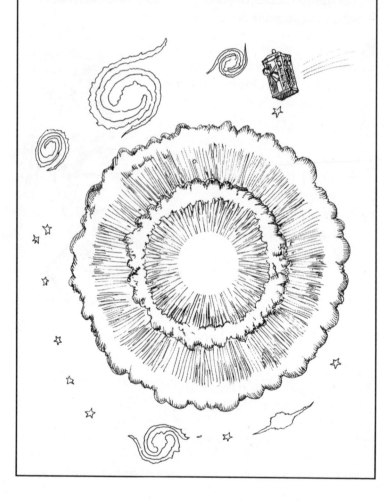

The Universe In A Nutshell

The Universe is often described as everything there is. Once upon a time, it was thought that it consisted of just the Sun, the Moon and a few planets and stars – all revolving around the Earth. This Earth-centred, or geocentric, view of things was formed during the time of the Ancient Greeks. It prevailed in Europe for almost 2,000 years until 1543, when the Polish astronomer, Nicholas Copernicus, described how the Earth and other planets revolved around the Sun.

Not-So-Crazy, Anaxagoras

Over 2,400 years ago, it's thought that the Ancient Greek philosopher, Anaxagoras believed the Earth was flat and was supported in space by 'strong air'. However, he was among the first to suggest that Earth orbited the Sun. He was thrown out of Athens for his crazy ideas!

Cosmologically Speaking

Cosmology is the science and study of the Universe as a whole – how it began, how it developed, its size, its shape and its future. Cosmologists delve into cutting-edge astronomy, physics and other sciences, as well as trying to think through and wrestle with major questions, such as 'How will the Universe end?', 'How did it get to where it is today?' and many other issues besides. You don't apply to become a cosmologist unless you have a very BIG brain!

115

Just When Was The Dawn Of Time?

Scientists estimate that the Universe is around 13.7 billion years old. It's a phenomenal period of time that's very hard to imagine and human beings have been around for just a tiny fraction of that period. In fact, if the Universe's entire history was condensed into 24 hours, the first homo sapiens – your fellow humans – arrived at less than two minutes to midnight.

The astronomer, Carl Sagan, made this point with his cosmic calendar by squeezing the entire Universe's history into a single Earth year:

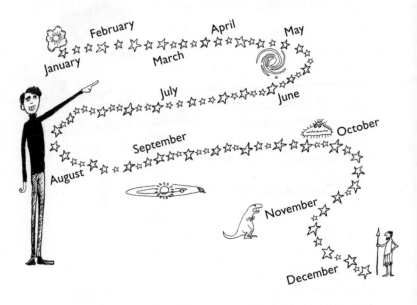

On Sagan's calendar, the Universe began forming on New Year's Day and the Milky Way only began to appear in May. The Sun and Solar System planets didn't start to form until September and human beings didn't arrive until the very last hour of 31st December.

So How Did It All Begin?

Most cosmologists agree that the Universe began in the way that is explained in the Big Bang theory. However, despite the name, it was never thought that the Universe began with a giant explosion. Instead, the theory describes how the Universe expanded suddenly from a single, unbelievably dense and hot point.

Who Called It The Big Bang Then?

Many people helped develop the Big Bang theory during the 20th century, including legendary big brain, Albert Einstein, as well as Edwin Hubble, George Gamow and a Belgian priest called Georges-Henri Lemaître. However, the theory got its name from a man who didn't actually agree with it! British astronomer, Fred Hoyle, first used the phrase, 'created in one big bang' on BBC radio in 1949, then repeated it in his 1950 radio lectures 'The Nature of the Universe'.

What Happened Next?

Space, energy and time all began with the Big Bang. As a result, there is no 'before' the Big Bang, but the very first tiny fraction of a second of the Big Bang itself is called the Planck Epoch after the Nobel Prize-winning scientist, Max Planck. People simply do not know what went on during this instant. After that, an incredibly sudden and rapid expansion called cosmic inflation occurred. This saw the Universe go from a single point to something huge in a fraction of a second! Ever since, the Universe has continued to expand, but has also cooled down, from millions of degrees to -270 °C today.

Around 380,000 years after the Big Bang, hydrogen and helium nuclei – the central bits of atoms – formed from protons and neutrons. Much later, electrons joined on to the nuclei to make atoms. A couple of other elements formed, while gravity began to pull gases and matter into clouds that heated up. The first stars and galaxies formed around a billion years after the Big Bang, but the Sun was a late arrival, forming around 7 billion years after that. All the time, the Universe continued to expand.

Amazing Ancients

In India, an ancient Hindu text named the *Rig Veda* described the Universe as a Cosmic Egg that expanded out of a single point. This sounds spookily like the Big Bang theory except the *Rig Veda* was written almost 3,500 years ago!

Steady On

Some scientists, including Fred Hoyle, who first used the phrase 'big bang', preferred what was known as Steady State theory. This said that stars and galaxies each had their own starting points, but the Universe did not – it had always existed and always would. Steady State theory was once very popular, but has been disproven.

Changing Light

One of the first people to detect the expanding Universe and to help form the Big Bang theory was the American astronomer, Edwin Hubble, in 1929. The Hubble Space Telescope (see pages 71 to 72) was named after him.

By observing light coming from galaxies, Hubble discovered that lots of galaxies were moving away from Earth and away from each other. The further a galaxy was from Earth, the faster it was racing away. To prove this, Hubble and his colleagues used the principle of 'redshift'. When a galaxy or another object moves quickly, it sends squashed-together light waves out in front of it, which are blue-ish in colour. Behind it, light waves are more stretched out and reddish. Human eyes cannot detect these colour changes, but an instrument called a spectrograph can. Distant galaxies from Earth show a clear redshift, proving that they are moving away at a speed of thousands of kilometres per second.

If the Universe has been expanding at a constant rate all along then, in the distant past, it must have been much smaller. The further back in time you go, the smaller the Universe would have been, until you get right back to the beginning when it must have been a single point.

Is The Universe Still Expanding?

Imagine the Universe is a delicious sultana scone – as the scone bakes, it expands in all directions. The sultanas, which were close together, move apart as the scone expands. Swap each sultana for a galaxy cluster and pretend the dough is the Universe. Although the Universe is not expanding *into* anything as it increases in size space itself is expanding as galaxy clusters move apart.

Prove It

More evidence for the Big Bang came in 1964, after two young scientists cleaned out the large radio antenna at Holmdel, New Jersey, which was full of pigeon droppings. Arno Penzias and Robert Wilson, who worked for Bell Laboratories, were hoping to use the antenna to monitor signals sent from early space satellites.

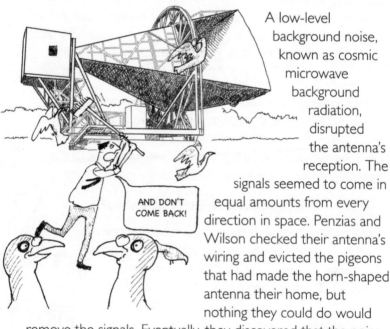

A low-level background noise, known as cosmic microwave background radiation, disrupted the antenna's reception. The signals seemed to come in equal amounts from every direction in space. Penzias and Wilson checked their antenna's wiring and evicted the pigeons that had made the horn-shaped antenna their home, but nothing they could do would remove the signals. Eventually, they discovered that the noise was actually energy left over from the Big Bang, which has spread with the Universe.

In 1978, the pair received the Nobel Prize for Physics for their discovery.

Remaining Questions

Astronomers and cosmologists are always learning more and more about the Universe, but lots of gaps in their knowledge remain. One mystery is the size and shape of the Universe.

Spherical?

Saddle-shaped?

Flat?

Doughnut-shaped?

I LIKE THE DOUGHNUT THEORY BEST.

The amount of the Universe that can be seen and measured by telescopes and other scientific instruments has increased as technology has advanced. It is now measured in tens of billions of light years. With the Universe expanding all the time though, the observed Universe may only be a part of the whole thing. Scientists also debate whether the Universe is 'finite' – meaning that it may have a definite, maximum size – or whether it is 'infinite' – meaning that it could be limitless.

What's The Matter?

Much of the Universe is missing! At least, that's what scientists think. By measuring how fast a galaxy spins, they have been able to work out just how much matter would be

needed to give the galaxy enough gravity to hold together. The problem is there doesn't seem to be enough matter. Either the law of gravity is wrong, which most scientists think is not the case, or there must be matter that reflects no light and can't be seen.

Scientists call this 'dark matter' and it is estimated to make up around 23 % of the Universe, but no one, as yet, knows what it's made of. It is possible that it is lots of brown-dwarf stars, black holes and particles with little or no mass, called neutrinos.

Scientists believe that the amount of dark matter in the Universe may determine how the Universe has developed and how, one day, it might end.

WHAT'S IN BETWEEN ALL THE STARS, MUM?

Dark Forces At Work

In the 1990s, another mysterious phenomenon was discovered at work in the Universe. It was a type of force that scientists believe is responsible for the Universe expanding at a quicker rate than expected. It was named dark energy although very little else is known about it. So far, people have not been able to measure it or fully understand what it consists of.

So How Will It All End?

No one knows for certain how the Universe will end, or if it will end at all. There are many possibilities that astronomers and cosmologists debate fiercely. Whatever the outcome, one thing that is certain is that it won't happen for a long, long time – trillions of years from now.

The Big Chill

Also known as the Big Freeze, this is one possible way that the Universe might end. The theory assumes that the Universe will continue to expand in all directions, for ever. The gaps between clusters of galaxies would get larger and larger as the galaxies grew older and older. Eventually, stars would exhaust their energy supplies and slowly die out, while galaxies would run out of gas and matter to form new stars. The Universe would continue to exist, but would be an impossibly vast, cold and dark place.

The Big Rip

This idea assumes that the Universe will continue expanding, but at a faster and faster rate, driven by dark energy (see opposite). As the Universe expands ever more quickly, a spectacular, terribly destructive ending could occur. Galaxies would no longer be able to hold themselves together, stars and planets would be torn apart and even individual atoms would be forced apart into their individual particles. Phut!

The Big Crunch

The Big Rip theory suggests that the expanding force of the Universe might overcome gravity, but what if gravity wins out? The Big Crunch theory is all about gravity gaining the upper hand. The Universe would stop expanding and, like an elastic band, shrink and pull in on itself. Galaxies would get closer and closer, before colliding and condensing inwards. Temperatures would soar and eventually the whole Universe would shrink into one unimaginably dense point, which is sometimes called the Big Crunch singularity.

Gulp!

This all sounds pretty gloomy, but there's trillions of years before any of this happens and lots more to discover about the Universe in the meantime.

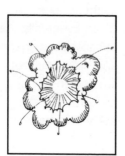

A Big Bounce?

If there was a Big Crunch, there is even the possibility that it wouldn't be the very end. It could result in a whole new Big Bang – the Big Bounce – and a brand new Universe could be created. It is also possible that a 'multiverse' of many universes exists, each created by their own Big Bang. Now there's an idea that is truly out of this world!

Index